D0903112

THE IDEA OF DEVELOPMENT OF THE SOUL IN MEDIEVAL JEWISH PHILOSOPHY

THE IDEA OF DEVELOPMENT OF THE SOUL IN MEDIEVAL JEWISH PHILOSOPHY

By

PHILIP DAVID BOOKSTABER, M.A., Ph.D., Litt.D.

Rabbi, Reform Temple Ohev Sholom,
Harrisburg, Penna.

PHILADELPHIA

Maurice Jacobs, Inc.

5711–1950

2nd Printing, 1950

PRINTED IN THE UNITED STATES OF AMERICA
PRESS OF Maurice Jacobs INC.
224 N. 15th ST., PHILADELPHIA 2, PENNA.

Dedicated to

MY DEAR CONGREGATION

OHEV SHOLOM

that made the publication of
this volume possible

CONTENTS

THE IDEA OF DEVELOPMENT OF THE SOUL IN MEDIEVAL JEWISH PHILOSOPHY

A POETIC FOREWORD

על הנשמה

חונה ונסגרת בבור גויה   מיום חנותה נצלה עדיה
רמה ותתחבר אלי־רמה   מי יערך דפיה לרב יפיה
יום פשטה הגוף אזי לבשה   עדיה והסירה כסות שביה
זורחה כשמש עלתה מבית   כלא נוה חשך ומאפליה
יצרה בשחק הללה כי־כן   כל הנשמה שם תהלל יה:

"THE SOUL"

JUDAH AL-HARIZI — Circa 1220

Translated by

REV. DR. VICTOR E. REICHERT

Rabbi, Rockdale Ave. Temple, Cincinnati, Ohio

In the cell of the body it lodges, confined
From the day of its dwelling, its jewels stripped bare;
Though exalted, yet with the worm it combined;
Can the body's defect to its beauty compare?
On the day that it puts off the body, it wears
Its jewels, removing earth's captive attire;
As the Sun going forth from a dungeon of pitch
It gleams through the darkness a flaming fire.
Its Maker it lauds in the heavenly skies
For there to praise God every soul vies!

NOTE: I have accepted the Hebrew text of Brody and Albrecht, Sha'ar Ha-Shir, (1906) p. 195. Line 5b — cf. Psalm 150:6. Brody and Albrecht fail, however, to indicate that the poet, Judah Al-Harizi, has spelled out his last name in the opening letters of the poem. I am glad to give this translation from my work on the *Taḥkemoni* of Harizi to my friend, Rev. Dr. Philip D. Bookstaber for his book on "Soul Development". The poem is from the Fiftieth Makama of the *Taḥkemoni.*

THE IDEA OF DEVELOPMENT OF THE SOUL IN MEDIEVAL JEWISH PHILOSOPHY

I.

PREFACE

He who attempts to write upon a subject such as the Soul is confronted with an embarrassment of correlated and subsidiary topics that tempt him to make the treatment encyclopaedic and voluminous. However, the guidance of teacher and experience have forced the author, after much research, to control his desire and ambition, for the present, and to limit the treatment of the "Soul" to a very few and well-chosen paths.

At the outset let it be understood that this book does not attempt to treat of the pre-existence of the Soul, nor of the Soul after death. These subjects may be touched upon only insofar as they must be mentioned in the development of the premise of the thesis.[1]

The treatment of the Soul in this thesis is further confined to certain writers of a given period — namely, the Medieval Period in Jewish philosophy.

Particular emphasis is placed upon the *development* of the *Soul.* This *is* my thesis. The thought may not be new but the treatment in its incipiency, I trust, may prove fruitful of more profound research in the future. I take the premise of Jeremiah[2] כי אם־איש בעונו ימות כל־האדם האכל הבסר תקהינה שניו: "But every one shall die for his own iniquity: every man that eateth the *sour grape, his teeth* shall be set on edge." It is of this implied potentiality of life and death within the individual that I choose to

[1] Surely am I not also acting in accordance with Mishna Ḥagigah Ch. 2. — "Whoever pries into four things had better not come into the world, namely: What is above and what is below, what was before and what will be after."

[2] Jer. 31.29.

treat, to point out how, consciously or unconsciously, the philosophers mentioned in this thesis failed or succeeded in attempting to explain the concept of Soul as a dynamic factor in positive living and thinking upon this earth. It is my thesis that Soul can be developed and that the individual may win or lose immortality of the soul insofar as he is willing to recreate within himself the divine spark which is ever-present within him in *potentia*. It is in this sense that the term "development" is used in this thesis. I am, by choice and agreement, however, limited to treat the subject of Soul of the philosophers given later and to leave my own view for the reflective analysis after each chapter. It has been a pleasure to assume the diligent task of research into this field — for, have I not thus been privileged to increase the content and the method of my own "Active Intellect"? The philosophers treated in this thesis, limited in number as they are, do indicate the importance of the concept of Soul as a motivating influence in life upon earth. I firmly believe that if people in general, people of all creeds, were given to understand the universal import of Jeremiah's utterance, and, couple it with the idea of potentiality and actuality and the possible results thereof, we would have a more rapid realization of the millenium.

The general and specific bibliographies are given, passim, in each chapter.

II.

INTRODUCTION

1. Soul-Concept — A Philosophy of Life.

When one is deeply interested in philosophy it falls to his lot now and then to grapple with the problem of his own philosophy of life.[1] Thus, the writer, after much reflection and reading, desires in this humble way to approach, or rather, intimate, what may be his philosophy of life in the years to come. In looking over the works of many philosophers, I find that they are always confronted with what seems to them and others the inevitable search for truth. To me the search for truth lies not in the intricate problems and discussions of God and immortality — (and the many other allied subjects) — for to me God exists and is made manifest through the *Soul* which is within me and goes from potentiality to actuality and thus its immortality is assured. The *Soul* — its nature and its function — gives one a key to a *true* philosophy of life and leads one to a fuller understanding of the world of the spirit. What have these seven philosophers, treated in this study, to say with regard to the Soul? How far does their treatment of the Soul affect their philosophy of life? How much "creativity"[2] do they attribute to the soul within man in attaining the realm of the Spirit? These are some of the questions to be answered in this research. The reader can now readily see the approach I am making to

[1] See Prof. Dr. David Neumark's masterly article on "Spirit" in *The Journal of Jewish Lore and Philosophy*, April, 1919, also *Rudolph Eucken — A Philosophy of Life*, by Abel J. Jones.

[2] "Creativity" is a term that I choose to use to denote the active and developmental part of man, in his desire to attain some ideal. In this treatise it relates particularly to the *soul*, with all its ramifications and meanings, as will be explained in the course of this inquiry. Note my Doctorate on *Creative Personality*, Stratford Co., Boston, 1925.

the solution of my philosophy of life, my "Weltanschauung." I deal with man of the present who, given a "soul" (for the present undefined) comes to a realization of his stewardship to the past and responsibility to the future and thus strives to fulfill his mission. Truly, many fall by the wayside — consciously or unconsciously — but this is a different problem. The *Soul* as an active force within man's life is the topic of chief concern — and to this, with some preliminary philosophical and historical considerations, we may now direct our attention.

2. *Historical Perspective*[3]

a) General and Arabic.

It is very necessary, in discussing any phase of Medieval Jewish philosophy, to give the sources and antecedents of influence with regard to the general field of religion and philosophy. Particularly is this imperative in the treatment of such a metaphysical subject as the Soul, about which the Greek and Arab thinkers had so much to say and, what they did say, influenced greatly the thinking of the Jewish philosophers. *Soul*, *reason*, and *intellect* are the terms used by all these philosophers; some use one or the other, or all three, separately or interchangeably; some give special emphasis to one as against the other two. These discussions formed a great part of philosophical study and research — it was a rationalistic approach[4] embodying an analysis of metaphysical, ethical and psychological problems and applying these studies to an interpretation of Scripture.

[3] In this chapter and all the following chapters I am indebted to the volumes of Prof. Dr. David Neumark on the History of Jewish Philosophy in the Middle Ages — *Geschichte der jüdischen Philosophie des Mittelalters, nach Problemen dargestellt*, Vols. I and II, Berlin, 1907 and 1910. Note Dr. Neumark's volume on תולדות הפילוסופיה בישראל, which gives in Hebrew much of the material referred to in this thesis.

[4] Here it may be intimated that Philo and Maimonides were not only the products of the Bible, Talmud and Jewish tradition alone, but that they combined Hebraism and Hellenism — Maimonides including still more — an Islamic philosophy.

The Jews of the Middle Ages fell heirs to both Greek and Arabic philosophy. Despite the closing of the Greek schools in Athens by Emperor Justinian the Greek influence was not abated. The West was intellectually barren and this was counter-balanced by the continual progress of Greek thought in Asia and Africa, not only since the closing of the schools[5] but even before then, due to the impress of the conquests of Alexander the Great in the Orient. Philosophy, medicine, and mathematics of the Greeks were studied and with the rise of Christianity the Greek influence became greater. Syria[6] was a center of Greek learning through the translations into Syriac of the great writers, such as Aristotle, Hippocrates, and Galen. After Christianity came Mohammedanism and, with it, a great revival of the study of the Greek philosophy and science. The Syrians of Greek learning and thought were courted by the Mohammedan Chieftans; the great Greek writers were translated into Syriac and then into Arabic. We thus see that Syrains were the mediators between the Greeks and the Arabs. This fact is important for our study, in that these Arabs became the teachers of the Jews, both of whom introduced Greek learning into Christian Europe about the 13th century.

In the foregoing we have the historical background that led up to the Arabic influence upon Jewish learning — The material, method, and terminology however, were all Greek with some inherent and evident accretions and changes. The outstanding figure, of course, is Aristotle — the organizer of thought and method and this influence was indelible. As will be pointed out, his (and also Plato's) ideas were not taken over entirely in their purity, for, the Arabic influence and the ignorance of the Greek original sources on the part of Jewish philosophers prevented such wholesome treatment. With few exceptions, we find that Aristotle, Plato, Arabic writers, Philo, and Plotinus, all left their impress upon the majority of thinkers and writers of the Middle Ages.[7] The earlier writers in Jewish

[5] 529 C. E.

[6] After it had become a Roman province in 64 B. C. E.

[7] The chief Arabic schools of influence may in brief be given as follows: Firstly came the school known as the "Kadariya" that sponsored free-will as

philosophy bear, unmistakably, the stamp of the Arabic influence and could easily be recognized because of the divisions of Unity of God and the Justice of God in their writings.[8] Not only in arrangement, but, to a great extent, in content, was the Arabic influence shown in the early Medieval Jewish writers on philosophy. The same subjects were treated — the discussions of substance and accident, the creation of God, of his attributes and justice, and of human free-will were handled in such a way that it was difficult to know whether the writer was Jewish or Arabic.

b) Greek.

The real beginning of the point of contact between Jewish and Greek philosophy and thought is within the third century when Alexander the Great goes from Palestine to the Orient. The question immediately arises as to what are the similarities and differences? Greek thought began opposite to Jewish thought (ethical in essence) in cosmological speculation. Hesiod is interested in cosmological questions — Homer — partly so. The Greeks were chiefly concerned with natural philosophy; in the material principle of the world and not primarily with the ethical or spiritual phases.

The Jews had a new God conception — namely — a spiritual — thus in great contrast and superior to the Egyptian

against the school of "Jabariya" that championed determinism. A third school arose in the Tenth Century called "Ashariya," a conciliatory group between strict orthodoxy and rationalism, who said that "God knows through a knowledge which is not different from his essence." A fourth school that had some influence upon Jewish philosophers (particularly, Bachya ibn Pakuda) is that of "the Sufis" — an ascetic group who adopted the doctrine of emanation so sponsored by the Neo-Platonic writers. From the first school and in opposition to the growth of Aristotelianism arose the school of "Mutakallimûn" who taught that Reason is the source of knowledge; they believed in creation of the world, individual providence, the reality of miracles. These thoughts, as is evident, are in contradistinction to the Aristotelians who believed in the eternity of motion, denied God's knowledge of particulars and insisted on the unchanging character of natural law.

[8] This was the standard division used by all Arabic writers.

ethical God conception. The Egyptians gave ethical ideas to such as Amos and the other prophets, but Jewish philosophy developed a new God conception. The Greek concern, as was intimated, was chiefly material. Numbers, as such, are for us, proportions for things. Pythagoras felt something of a spiritual force in numbers they are the "form principle." This may be called the initial step in the spiritual idea — yet none of the philosophers before Socrates and Plato understand the "Spirit idea" of the Eleatic School. Parmenides had actually said "Being — existence, and thinking are the same thing" and thus we have a distinct approach of the spiritual idea. Yet, the Eleatic School did not attempt to explain the world of nature — the world of becoming; it just recognized *being* but did not explain spiritual. Their opponents — the School of Heraclitus,[9] — did not even recognize *change* and, in this, they opposed the spiritual idea. Democritus is entirely material. Empedocles, in addition to the four principles of nature, recognizes also the two non-material factors — love and hate — yet treat them as mythological, not spiritual principles. Anaxagoras was the first to introduce the spiritual. He opposes Heraclitus in two essentials, namely, in his view of a dynamism with a mechanical cosmogony and secondly, Anaxagoras substitutes dualism for hylozoistic monism by assuming the existence of an unintelligent principle, the cause of motion. To this Socrates directs criticism, for, he says, Anaxagoras did not direct this spiritual principle towards man. This is the first step which reminds us of Jewish thought, that is, they became interested in ethical questions with the spiritual principle in back of it all.

Plato's theory of ideas had something in common with Jewish thought and philosophy. This is the problem of "the one and the many." Plato, as well as Judaism, raises the question: How can we explain the many things out of one principle? For example; Every man represents the same thing and yet so different, why? Because of the development of varieties,

[9] In this connection I should like to refer the reader to the erudite study made by Dr. Henry Slonimsky entitled "Heraclites and Parmenides" in German (Giessen, 1912, particularly, pp. 15 and 31).

of species. This is a point of contact with Jewish thought. For example — the subject of angelology is a phase of the discussion of the "one in the many." Strict monotheists did not believe in angels and the reason why men did believe in angels was because of the prevailing pluralism. Today, even, many philosophers believe in polytheism because they see so many conflicting powers and forces in the world. It is claimed that Plato got his theory of ideas from Oriental sources — Egypt. Plato combines this theory with that of Pythagoras. Aristotle, though against Plato, calls himself a disciple. However, the oldest source of the "theory of ideas" is Babylonian. For example, before God created *the* or *a* tree here He had a heavenly tree as a model. The Babylonians had sanctuaries which they fashioned after heavenly patterns. Plato comes near to this idea when he says that there are heavenly entities, incorporeal, after which man etc. are patterned — The heavenly entities are mirrored in man and the differences are due to the fact that this principle must work on matter and matter has a passive resistance as the products of many sculptors using the same pattern yet working on different pieces of matter will be different. Thus, there is one man, yet being fused with matter makes many differences. The "P" code gives this view before Plato ever had it — e. g. The Tabernacle being patterned after the heavenly one.[10] The Jews had this principle — ethical and not philosophical in content. Thus there was a point of contact in the beginning of the third century. Judaism has an ethical background with a cosmological superstructure with the "Theory of Ideas" standing out with all of its importance. Plato looms forth as the only one outside of the fold of Judaism who had ethical enthusiasm as great as that of the Jewish prophets — his enthusiasm (ethical) is the acme and epitome of Greek ethics.

With this contact it is not surprising that Jewish thought was influenced by Greek thought. The Jews took from the Greeks their "levity," but, also, adopted much of their philosophy. The literature, historical and philosophical, show in many divers ways how intense this influence was. Plato and Aristotle

[10] Note also Rabbinic and Midrashic references to תבנית.

stand forth as leaders, varying in prominence at different periods. The questions rightfully are asked, why were the Jews at first more inclined to be influenced by Plato as against Aristotle? The answer is, because the Jews found themselves "at home" in Plato. The Jews were not prepared for Aristotle — he was too logical, whereas Plato was the poetic philosopher and more in harmony with the Jewish experience and feelings. Later on when the Jews became more "dialectical," during the Middle Ages, then they could undertake, understand, and appreciate Aristotle.

c) Periods:

Many classifications of the literary products of the past may be made with regard to the development of Jewish philosophy, but the most feasible is the following:

(1) The Biblical Period
(2) The Alexandrian Period
(3) The Graeco-Jewish Period
(4) The Talmudic Period
(5) The Gaonic Period
(6) The Classical Period of Jewish Philosophy

It is not our province to go into a detailed description of any of the above periods.[11] There are, however, some salient philosophical features that can, in brief, be brought out.[12]

To begin with we may rightfully say that the concepts of "Ma'ase Bereshit" and "Ma'ase Merkabah" begin our Jewish philosophy. They are not new nor limited to any particular period. We find these two ideas of philosophic speculation in Ezekiel[13] and the *P* code; we find them in the first and third periods mentioned above. The Talmud itself is a source to the effect that the Bible has an esoteric as well as a literal meaning.[14] We find a reference there to a mystic doctrine of creation known

[11] The post-Maimonidean period need not be discussed, but only be referred to in this thesis.

[12] The soul concept of these periods will be treated separately.

[13] Chapters 1 and 10.

[14] Talmud Babli Ḥagigah 11b.

as "Ma'ase Bereshit" and a doctrine of the divine chariot called "Ma'ase Merkabah." The Mishna, however, ignores these two ideas and deals only with cosmological questions until Jochanan ben Zakkai[15] permitted discussion of "Ma'ase Merkabah" and Akiba did likewise with "Ma'ase Bereshit" in the Talmud. With these sanctions authoritative Judaism allowed discussions of the hitherto prohibited fields of speculation.[16] Palestine was the seat of mystical speculation and when the center of Judaism was transplanted to Babylonia we find a change in Jewish thought and speculation with Rab at the head. His emphasis was upon the "theory of ideas" insisting upon the principle of creation which was irreconcilable with the "theory of ideas" according to the Grecian and Roman philosophers. It is natural, also to see here, Philo's influence, particularly in Rab's enlargement upon the conception of "Ma'ase Bereshit" of R. Akiba, of which he himself was a great exponent. It is here that the dialectical method reached its zenith — the height of the fifth, the Gaonic period — and paved the way for the influence and acceptance of Aristotle. Alongside with this beginning of Aristotelian influence must be mentioned the fact that after the redaction of the Talmud (c. 550) we find a reappearance of מ"מ and מ"ב and at about the ninth century we find a reappearance of the "system of ideas" in the treatise of "ספר יצירה" "Book of Creation."[17] Rab's influence is here evident. Many of the first philosophic writings of the Middle Ages were commentaries to the "ספר יצירה" — the "Book of Creation." This Book also became the basis of the Medieval mystical speculation known as the Kabbala — its influence upon Jewish philosophy is incomparable to any other

[15] This he did in order to meet the Christians on their own ground and destroy its stand. See David Neumark, *Philosophy of the Bible*, pp. 291–298, for a fuller discussion of this subject. It may be stated here that later the discussions of מ"מ and מ"ב were dropped because Christianity ceased to be an important item and that the discussions of the "Halacha" took the place of those related to מ"מ and מ"ב. The only exception is Rabbi Yehuda ben Elai.

[16] Talmud Babli Ḥagigah 11b.

[17] This is not surprising for the Mishna itself, with Rab's influence added thereto, brought about a new point of crystallization. The underlying "motif" of the Mishna was that *everything* is created — whether מ"מ, מ"ב or the "system of ideas."

treatise. The high development of the method, and the dialectical philosophy in particular, was due largely to two factors, namely, the new contact of the Jews with Greek philosophy, (Aristotle); (this being evolved from Syrian and Arabic Schools as explained previously) and secondly, to the Karaitic movement. This sect, attacked the Merkabah doctrines of the Talmudists for their anthropomorphic God conception in order to break down the people's faith in Talmudic tradition. This sect joined the Arabic liberal School of Mu'tazila, whose doctrine was based upon the "theory of ideas" as against the orthodox Arabic school that emphasized the doctrines based on the Merkabah.[18] This conflict forced a change in the "Rabbinites" and philosophy and rational interpretation was their recourse. The "Merkabah" and the "theory of ideas" were rejected. Aristotle (his "Physics") was their mentor and the group known after the leader Saadya (892–942) developed a philosophy devoid of all mysticism. However, about two hundred years later, in the West, there arose a group, a school, after Gabirol (1021–1070) who adopted Aristotle's mysticism (his "Metaphysics" and the Arabic Neo-Platonists) and brought forth speculations of a deep and complex group, a school, after Gabirol (1021–1070) who adopted Aristotle's mysticism (his "Metaphysics" and the Arabic Neo-Platonists) and brought forth speculations of a deep and complex nature.[19] It became Maimonides' (1135–1204) task to unite the best and most authoritative elements of both these schools

[18] Both these schools, according to Dr. David Neumark, have built up their theories under Jewish influence. The Jews contributed much and are not given credit therefore, because the Arabs were in power and made it impossible for such recognition. The Jews did get method from the Arabs.

[19] As to these schools — Dr. Neumark traces a continuity in philosophical thought and influence from מ"מ to Ezekiel, then to Gabirol, the metaphysicist to dualism. Likewise, for the other group — from מ"ב to Jeremiah then to Saadia, the physicist, to Monism. He says (*op. cit.*, pp. 300–301): "But the foregoing will suffice to confirm our general thesis that the development of Jewish thought in biblical times was decisively preformative and forcefully directive for all future developments. Historical events and relations continously brought new elements and new motifs in the evolution of thought, but the basic tendencies of the spiritual currents in speculative thoughts and cultural manifestations remained the same. And this can be shown also of the essential formations of modern times."

and bring about the supremacy of reason in all religio-philosophical speculations.

3. *Main Features of Medieval Jewish Philosophy.*

With the above historical background we are now able to undertake a brief review of the content of the philosophical discussions in Medieval times. This becomes more necessary here, because, when the individual philosophers treated in this thesis are taken up, I must be limited to only one phase of their writings — namely — the *Soul.*

There are certain theories that all of them treated to a greater or lesser extent depending upon the period and persons of influence. These may, in a summary way, be here given.

As was stated above, Plato (and Neo-Platonism) and Aristotle affected the thinking of the Jew as well as having transformed their religious and ethical discussions into metaphysical systems. The point of view heretofore of the relationship of God to man and to nature was distinctly personal, human, teleological and ethical — and this was given a metaphysical turn which assumed four distinctive bases, namely, the "theory of ideas," the theory of emanation, the doctrine that matter is a form principle of evil and agnosticism. The common or universal element in nature was sought after; method, through description and definition, applied a thorough research into the discussions of the questions of *change* which, it was agreed, implies an unchanging substratum which is Matter not affected by quality or form. The whole discussion of *Matter* and *Form*, *Motion*, *Potentiality* and *Actuality*, and, relating these to the attributes of God, to man and nature was thrashed out by many philosophers of this period. The world of matter was put into contrast with the world of the spirit giving rise to the speculations upon the subjects of natural and ethical laws. God was "impersonalized, "He was not corporeal, He is pure form and thought, He is thought, thinking thought. The world of matter, the sublunar world, is subject to generation and decay; all things are destined to change; nothing is permanent and, destruction of one thing is the genesis of another — there is no annihilation.

The above discussion bears particularly now upon our subject of *soul* — for in man's soul we find a *form* which combines within itself characteristics of the worlds of matter and spirit, the sublunar and celestial forms.[20] When it is in contact with the body it performs and exhibits activities through matter as other sublunar forms and is inseparable from matter. Death does not destroy it for it continues separately in form afterwards. The Jewish philosophers were much concerned with the concept of Soul and the one just intimated had much to do with their speculations — and — particularly, with those writers covered in this treatise.

The Greek influence in the soul-classification[21] is important. — The Jewish philosophers vary from the Platonic view that the soul is a distinct entity coming into the body from a spiritual world, and acting *in* the body by using the latter as its instrument — to the Aristotelian view that, at least, so far as the lower faculties are concerned, — the *soul* is the *form* of the body, and disappears with the death of the latter. The human unit is one of body plus mind; the activities are psycho-physical and not as Plato would have it purely psychical. The Arabic influence (essentially Aristotelian) gave us the concept of "Active Intellect"[22] — sense experience — through this active intellect — is converted into immaterial concepts — and these constitute the immortal part of man. In this relation we have Aristotle's idea of potential intellect which has both a passive and an active phase, the former dies with the body and the latter is immortal. Close to Aristotle's influence is that of Plotinus. Aristotle's gradations of Being are static and in Plotinus they are dynamic.[23] Aristotle's, to be sure, is theistic and dualistic while Plotinus is

[20] See Yalkut Shimeoni: אמר רבי חייא בר אבא: הנשמה שבאדם — בכל שעה היא עולה ויורדה, והיא מבקשת לצאת ממנו. והיאך היא עומדת בגופו? אלא הקב"ה כבודו מלא עולם, והיא באה לצאת ורואה את יוצרה וחוזרת לאחוריה. לכן: ,,כל הנשמה'' — כל־זמן שהיא עולה ויורדת — ,,תהלל יה'' — על הפלאים שהוא עושה עמנו.

[21] The commonest classification of Soul is into vegetative, animal, and rational. Plato's is appetitive, spiritual, and rational.

[22] The thoughts of this "Active Intellect" have become the realities for many philosophers — cf. the "Logos" of Philo and Augustine and Maimun's *Moreh Neb.*, Ch. III, 18. A fuller discussion of acquired and active and other intellects will be taken up with the philosophers dealing with same.

[23] It is this "dynamicity," this creativity, which forms the major part of my inquiry into what I call the "development" of the soul.

pantheistic and monistic. The three hypostases of Plotinus, namely, Being, "nous" or Reason, and "World Soul," proceed in descending order as given — this process, this development, if I may so call it, has been unknowingly adopted by our philosophers as Aristotelian and much has been made of it. Truly, it is a valuable contribution, for, it again emphasizes the importance of the "creativity," the dynamicity of man's soul. True, man's body is material and therefore partakes of the evil of matter, — but his soul comes from, — emanates from, — the "World Soul" to the intelligible and sensible world and partakes of both — if his Soul strives for perfection it will, after the death of the body return to its abode in the intelligible world. As to God, He is the acme of perfection. He is absolutely unknowable and of Him negations are only true. Such ideas are foreign to Aristotle and are indicative of Philo's influence; this is expressed, too, in ibn Daud, and Maimuni applies this in his classical solution of the problems of the attributes of God.

Brief, as the above is, of the content of Medieval Jewish philosophy, we can see that the topics of *Soul*, reason, or intellect, form an important part of the discussions of these great thinkers. It remains for us, before taking up the individual writers, to close this chapter with a brief survey of the various terms used in our Hebrew literature.

4. *The Term* Soul *in Hebrew Literature.*[24]

Throughout the conflict of philosophic thought the question of *Soul* has held no mean place — it is because here and there, individuals and groups have made it the kernel and the center of their systems of thought. Judaism, it may truthfully be said, does not consider the *Soul* as the exclusive citadel of the divine as opposed to the body. — Judaism admits no complete dualism of spirit and matter — the whole human personality is divine to the extent of which it moulds and develops itself toward a divine end. The Rabbis have thus sanctified the body as well

[24] For a summary discussion, see Schmiedl, A., *Studien über jüdische, insbesonders jüdisch-arabische Religionsphilosophie*, Wien, 1869, pp. 129–167.

as the mind[25] and have gone further in trying to connect even all natural phenomena with the Torah so as to emphasize a complete continuity — *one* Law — a monism, if you please. The Greek idea that man is a *microcosm* reflecting the whole cosmos was frequently expressed and emphasized[26] — man bears the stamp of divinity and manifests it by the creativity on his part to elevate the realm of the senses, the flesh, matter, into the sphere of morality and holiness.

We see, however, from the above that man does possess a dual nature the flesh — "basar"[27] and the spirit — the "breath of God" the "Ruah Elohim." The latter is the *form principle* that makes the flesh a living being — the רוח חיים, penetrates all living creatures at whose departure the living creature becomes lifeless. This רוח חיים is possessed by animal as well as by man, hence, in ancient times the terms "breath," רוח and "soul" נפש or נשמה were used as synonymous.[28] Later on the correlation of soul and "blood" דם, was made manifest since man and beast both die when the life-blood flows out of the body. —[29] Thus both man and beast possess a soul — נפש — that of man is distinguished by a greater and special endowment — a creativity[30] — the רוח lifts man into a higher realm and makes him a free moral personality.

The terms נפש, נשמה, and רוח[31] in the Bible proper are used

[25] See R. Hillel's comparison in Lev. R. 34:3. Apropos, this we may say that the Talmudic philosophy throughout derives its God conception from a comparison of the soul with body. The Greek influence here, of course, is most evident.

[26] Ab. deR. N., 31.

[27] The term "all flesh" is used for both man and beast, see Gen. 6.12, 19.

[28] The Latin *anima* and *spiritus* and the Greek *pneuma* and *psyche.*

[29] Gen. 9.21. Lev. 17.11, 14.

[30] See *Commentary* to Gen. 2.7, particularly in re: וייצר.

[31] See Dillman, *Gen. Com.*, 355–361; A. B. Davidson, *Gen. Com.*, 182–203; comp. Gen. R. 14:11, where these three terms are given and also יחידה, Ps. 22.21; 35.17 and חיה Ps. 143.3; Job 33.1; see also Yalkut Eliezer, division of נשמה for many references and amplifications. Also, in Chapter 8. See Saadia's *Emunoth Vedeoth*, pp. 153–154. In ספר תורות הנפש by Pseudo-Bahya (translated by Broyde into French from the Arabic under title: "Les Reflexions sur l'ame par Bahya ben Joseph ibn Pakuda" 1896) we find ten names by which soul is known. In the Zohar (see ספרא דצניעותא) *soul* has a two-fold division —

synonymously and coterminously. Philo, adopting the Platonic division, gives a three-fold classification as above.[32] The Jewish philosophers of the Middle Ages, beginning with Saadia, made similar divisions knowing well that the classification of Soul into three substances had no scriptural warrant.[33] The Rabbis, however, emphasize the term נשמה, as the human *psyche*, the higher spiritual substance, and the contrast thereto is not the Biblical בשר, flesh, but the Aramaic גוף, "Guph," body.[34] They recognized no relationship between the soul of the animal and that of man — man has a special type of existence — *God* causes the soul to enter the body[35] and this pre-existence of the soul was shared both by Rabbis and Philo with the Apocryphal authors.[36] The Rabbis, it must be borne in mind, never emphasized the fact as Philo and Plato and the Paulinian System did, that the body or the flesh was the source of impurity and sin or "the prison house of the soul." The Rabbis recognized a "tendency" a יצר, but never a compulsion toward sin. Man has the divine power, the freedom, to overcome the evil (יצר הרע)[37] by the good (יצר הטוב) inclination and the greatest men in history are those who can control (and have controlled) the passions within their souls.[38] Our Medieval philosophers, influenced by the Greeks, adopted the theory, that there is a substance of souls — "Nefesh Haḥiyoonith" נפש החיונית — the basic life-

namely, נשמתא קדישא, the higher or Sabbath Soul, and הנפש השכלית, the lower, or week-day Soul. In re: Soul and Spirit, see Guttmann, J., *Die Philosophischen Lehren des Isaak ben Solomon Israeli*, Münster in W., 1911, *l. c.*, and notes, pp. 49–50. Israeli, Book of Def., p. 138: ואמרו כי הנפש היא עצם רוחני יחד.

[32] De Leg. Alleg. 3:38.

[33] See Horovitz, *D. Psychologie Saadias*; *Scheyer*, *D. Psycholog. System d. Maimonides*; Cassel's *Cuzari*, pp. 382–400.

[34] Sanh. 91a, b; Nid. 30b–31b; Sifre Deut. 306, ref. to Deut. 32.1; Lev. 4.5–8.

[35] Ab. Zarali. 5a; Gen. B. 8:1.

[36] B. Wisdom 8:20; Slav. Enoch 23:5; Philo 1:15, 32; 2:356, comp. Baresset *l. c.*, pp. 508 ff.

[37] Gen. 6.5; 8.21; B. Sira 15:14; 17:31; 21:11; Ber. 5a; Kid. 30b; Suk. 52a, b. Shab. 152b; Eccl. R. 12:7; comp. F. Ch. Porter: "The Yezer ha-Ra" in *Biblical and Semitic Studies*, pp. 93–156; Bourset, *l. c.*, 462 f.

[38] Suk. 52a, b.

principle (the form-principle) of men and animals.[39] With this inherent and potential unique characteristic, man stands in the very center of the universe and God esteems him "equal in value to the entire creation."[40] The soul, to most of our Jewish philosophers of Medieval times, is divested of every sensory attribute and portrayed as a divine power within the body. We are now ready to undertake a full discussion of the way in which our Medieval Jewish philosophers treated the subject of *soul* — bearing in mind the emphasis and limitations of this thesis.

[39] Truly this is an anticipation of modern physiological and psychological discoveries. Our Rabbis have, in their discussions, adopted the tri-partite soul division of Plato, reason, passion and courage and Aristotle's, reason, perception and nutrition (Philo gave also a twofold division, rational, and irrational). However, because of a desire to correlate the soul division with the cardinal virtues on a functional basis they (like Plato and Philo) call wisdom חכמה, courage גבורה, and temperance, עושר, (also: to צדק) justice being the harmonization of the three (see Ab. Zarali Ch. 10, Tanh. Bemidbar Mattoth, comp. Babli Ḥagigah 12a). From this the Rabbis get their God conception and say that He is the sum of the cardinal virtues and the form principle of the soul.

[40] Thus says Rabbi Nehemiah of a single human soul (Ab. deR. N. 31).

III.

ISAAC BEN SOLOMON ISRAELI

1. *Life and Works.*

Israeli was the first dialectic philosopher. He was born in Egypt and from there he went to Kairuan to assume the position of court physician to several Caliphs. His dates are 855–955. His works do not rank him as a great philosopher — for he expounded no new system nor did he give any solutions to anything specifically Jewish. In his day he must have been highly respected as a great physician. His works are purely of an eclectic nature. He shows Aristotelian and Platonic influences. His merit lies in the fact that he directed the attention of the Jews of his day to the study of the science and philosophy of the Greeks.

The works of interest and importance to us are the following: "Book of the Elements"[1] and the "Book of Definitions."[2] These were in Arabic.[3] In the first book he is primarily concerned with the problems of physics, of nature — namely the definition of an element — and, he follows this up with the inquiry as to the number and character of the elements and of which the sublunar world is made. The Book is nothing more nor less than a Jewish elaboration of Aristotle's "Physics." The elements are four,

[1] S. Fried, *Das Buch über die Elemente*, ספר היסודות, Drohobycz, 1900.

[2] Published by Hirschfeld in *Festschrift zum achtzigsten Geburtstag Moritz Steinschneiders*, Leipzig, 1896, pp. 131–141; cf. also 233–4.

[3] The complete list of his works, in addition to the above, are as follows:
- a) A commentary to Sefer Yetzirah — in Arabic.
- b) ספר הרוח והנפש — published by Steinschneider in the Hebrew periodical הכרמל I (1872), pp. 401–5.
- c) An article on מאמר ישרצו המים, in Hebrew, by Senior Sachs in *Literaturblatt des Orients*, XI, p. 166, and in "התחיה" (Berlin, 1850), p. 39.

namely, fire, air, water, earth, and he then discusses many other items of physics, physiology, logic and psychology. In this book he adopts much of Galen and Hippocrates. He refutes the Atomic theory, he gets away from Aristotle on certain points.

2. *The Soul.*

For our purpose we may say that in his definition of an element he touches upon soul. He says that an element is an ingredient; it enters into composition; every one of the four elements is a last element; you can't analyze it. On the other hand, the soul is the highest composite.[4] Take one of the last elements, e. g. air, and the highest composite — *soul* — and know its process. — We need not ask why and what: it is self-explanatory. — The intensive qualities *create* the extensive qualities.[5]

The other, the "Book of Definitions" gives us a fuller discussion of some philosophical problems. Here he defines and describes such terms as intelligence, science, philosophy, soul, spirit, nature, etc. To know one's self is to understand his spiritual as well as his corporeal phases of life — and thus one knows everything. The Soul and the reason are spiritual; the body with its three dimensions is corporeal.[6] The study of science leads one to a full knowledge of reality, and one of these great realities is the purpose of the union of body and soul. Who knows this purpose can realize what is truth, what is good, and thus he will receive from the Creator the reward which consists in clinging to the *upper soul*,[7] and in thus attaining spirituality and perfection. To attain the realm of the upper soul one must

[4] Books of Elements — Hebrew, p. 68; Latin, Fol. X, Col. 1.

[5] In this he anticipates and refutes Descartes in re extension and thinking

[6] Guttmann, J., *l. c.*, p. 25 and note.

[7] Israeli has the three-fold division of soul; rational, animal and vegetative, each successively emanating from "A Splendor," and "Intelligence" by God. The Splendor and the rational soul are both permanent and fixed, the others are not. Although the three souls are cosmic and not individual, still the principle of individuation occurs in the sub-lunar world. It is this individuation which I like to stress; it is this developmental phase that Israeli emphasized too. See his Liber definit., Heb., pp. 136–138.

strive to overcome his animal pleasures and desires — one must *work*[8] himself out of potentiality to actuality. This "participation" of the individual in the cosmic soul process is what makes the individual and his efforts so important. The rational soul strives to appropriate more and more of the first intelligence[9] obtaining a complete identity — spiritual in nature.

The question of soul has been a perpetual puzzle to the philosophers of all times. Some thought it was a material substance, others understood it to be purely spiritual; is soul substance or accident? To Israeli the soul is not an accident but a substance.[10]

3. *Reflective Analysis.*

From the limited and intensive study of the soul, we may, at present pause and reflect upon the element of "Creativity" in Israeli's discussion. I do not want to read into the utterances of this eclectic philosopher, but, I do appropriate for my own reflection certain elements which have not been brought to mind or emphasized in this light.

[8] Book of Def., Heb., p. 132. והחקיקה הלקוחה מחוקתה היא כי הפילוסופיא נדמה לבורא ית' לפי כח האדם. See Guttmann, *l. c.*, p. 21 and note.

[9] Israeli divides Intelligence into three classes: actual, potential and the second intelligence i. e. the sense impressions — the *phantasia* — See Book of Def., Hebrew, p. 135; Latin, Fol. II, Col. 4: Also Guttmann, *l. c.*, pp. 36–37. We see in this the Aristotelian classification of intellect in active and passive. Israeli adds what Aristotle omitted, namely, the process of realization from the passive into the active state. See Neumark's Vol. I, p. 413. Israeli gets away from the Greek point of view which postulates *change* and never *Being*. Matter, is, he says, is because it is; every form exists because it exists שהוא כאלו נותן לגופות שמותן ותכליתן והיה כל אחד מהגופות נקרא הוא מה שהוא.

[10] Using substance and accident in the purely logical and ontological sense. His discussion is in Book of Elements: Hebrew, p. 12 ff. Cf. Aristotle's definition of Soul in De Anima II 412a; 27, Lat., Fol. V, Col. I. In Book of Def. Heb. p. 136 and Latin Fol. III Col. 1. He refers to Plato's definition as follows: ואמר אפלטון הנפש היא עצם מתחדש [מתאחז] בגוף וגו'. Latin — et dixit Plato: anima est substantia corpori et peristam unionem etc. With regard to the soul, being Form, and not an accidental product of the corporeal world, see also Book of Elements, Hebrew, p. 68; Lat., Fol. X, Col. 1. Cf. Saadia's Emunot, ch. VI; Aristotle, De Anima, I, 494b, 8.

I want to herewith discuss reflectively his idea of emanation.[11] Truly, it is Neo-Platonic — almost Plotinus in toto. — The successive radiations, from the main source of light, (Truth, Goodness, Splendor, God, Intelligence) diminish in spirituality until the Sphere — הגלגל, is reached wherein the things are material and visible to the physical senses. The relationship between the cosmic hypostases (the Intelligence)[12] and the three souls[13] and the rational and psychic faculties in man, Israeli does not explain. I may venture to say that since God did create the Splendor (ברא השם בהירא) and sent out a "spark" (ניצוץ) that this spark is the nervating force in his whole scheme of emanation — this spark is dormant in many individuals; it is ready to bring them from the sphere to the cosmic hypostases with a distinct individuality. The *sphere* is the mid-way house, so to speak, between the world of intelligence and the corporeal world of the world of elements. The spark which an individual can appropriate, which he can kindle into rationality and consciousness, is there. The process is both ascending and descending, but for man it is the former. — He may proceed from the elements to the sphere, through the cosmic hypostases and then to the Splendor. Israeli claims that the power of the rational soul (כח הנפש המשכלת) which is permanent and fixed emanates from the Splendor, (הבהירות) and then there proceeds a descending order of emanation. But, we individuals, through a process of time, have within us, almost intuitively (through creation) a divine spark that, immediately after birth, puts us into touch with the world of Intelligence, of Splendor, of God. *We* can emanate out of the Shadow, the dimness, the materialism of our earthly existence.

The second point I choose to emphasize is the use that Israeli makes of the Aristotelian doctrine of potentiality and actuality

[11] See ha-Karmel, *l. c.*, Vol. I, pp. 401; 403–404; for exact Hebrew text with notes for this statement. Also see Guttmann, J., *l. c.*, note 1, pp. 31–32 for Hebrew and corrections. German translation of these passages.

[12] In re: the Souls and Intelligence, see Book of Def., Heb., p. 136; Latin, Fol. III, Col. 1. והעולה לנפשות למעלה הגדולה היא מעלת הנפש השכלית שהיא בקו הדעה ומצלה נולדה.

[13] Book of Def., Heb., p. 136; Lat., Fol. III, Col. 1; Book of El., Heb., p. 57; Lat., Fol. IX, Col. 2, Commentary to Sefer Yezirah, pp. 60–70.

referred to above.[14] This discussion was one with which all the philosophers had to contend. Israeli introduces an intermediate stage in his classification of Intelligences.[15] — True it is there is a *potential* and actual intelligence, but there is an intermediary stage — namely — a *process* of realization of the potential (or passive) intellect through the sense stimuli on the one hand and the influence of the active intellect on the other. In short, the individual has, *intuitively* — certain intellectual and spiritual potentialities and it remains for him to so use his gifts, wisely and justly[16] so as to bring about an actuality of his faculties; to so re-create within himself the latent and inherent energies that "a high type of *soul*," (the rational soul) could be consummated and thereby be put into communion with God — with Truth — with the realm of Spirit.

[14] Guttmann, J., *l. c.*, pp. 36–37; Book of Def., Hebrew, p. 135; Latin, Fol. II, col. 4.

[15] Namely "phantasia" referred to above — ולכן חלק הפילוסוף הדיעה שלשה חלקים. ה א ח ת: הדיעה שהוא בפועל תמיד והוא אשר הקדמנו באמרנו, כי מינות הדברים עמה לפנים תמיד. ו ה ש נ י ת: הדיעה אשר בנפש בכח קודם יציאתה אל הפועל. וכשתודע יצא מה שהיה בתוכה מהכח אל הפועל כמו דיעת הילד, שהיא בו בכח, וכשיגדל וילמד וידע, יצא מה שיש בו מן הכח אל הפועל ויהיה חכם. ו ה ש ל י ש י: היא כאשר נחקק בידיעה השנית — ותוליכה הפנטסיאה אל נפש השכל, וכשתכירה הנפש תעשה היא והם דבר אחד כסברה הרוחנית לא כנושמנית. ולכן חקק הפילוסוף זה המין מזו הדיעה מהדיעה השנית. כי הוא מתחיל [מההרגש ועולה] מעלה מעט מעט ומדריגה, עד שיגיע בדיעה אשר תצא בנפש מהכח אל הפועל.

[16] In this connection I refer the reader to Guttmann's fine exposition of this idea — what I choose to call "creativity." — individual in essence and not cosmic in nature — Guttmann, J., *l. c.*, pp. 48–49 and note thereto: Book of Elements, Hebrew, p. 57; Latin, Fol. IX, Col. 2.

IV.

SAADIA BEN JOSEPH AL-FAYYUMI (892–942)

1. *Life and Works.*

With Saadia begins the first important presentation of Jewish philosophy — a systematic dissertation upon the vital questions in Judaism is given by him. Saadia is the incarnation of Jewish life and thought up to his day. This is evident because, in his day, the Mishna and the Talmud had been long completed and these two were the great fountain springs of Judaism. As head of the academy at Sura, the center of Jewish learning, he was the heir to all that passed before him in the development of Jewish lore, teaching, and philosophy — his was the unique heritage — to interpret and to teach that which was handed down to him by lawgiver, prophet, scribe, Pharisee, Tanna and Amora, Saburai and Gaon. It was to the good fortune of the Jews that Saadia did come as head of Sura at a time fraught with dissension, strife and agitation in the intellectual ranks of both Jew and Islamite.

Various schools arose in Islam[1] as well as in Judaism, seeking for new interpretations and new alignments in the problems of faith, science, life and tradition. Saadia proved himself equal to the task of directing the dissenters "of the vast multitudes" giving power to the faint of heart and to those that had no might he increased them with strength.[2] Saadia met the attacks of the Karaites and corrected and systematized Jewish thought. He was a true philosopher; — Israeli an eclectic. His was the task to give a good foundation to the Hebrew extant in his day and he set about it by paying attention to grammar and lexicography; he was the first to translate the Bible into Arabic

[1] See Introductory Chapter.
[2] Is. 40.29.

and the first to write a commentary thereto. Saadia's greatest task was to write a system of philosophy that was to be in harmony with the traditions in Judaism and, at the same time, be in accord with the philosophic and scientific opinion of the day. The result was the treatise that made Saadia's name immortal; his "chef d'oeuvre," entitled "Emunot ve-Deot," "Beliefs and Opinions."[3] The work is a Mu'tazilite model — having the two characteristic divisions of *Unity* and *Justice*.

The volume has ten chapters and the subjects treated cover the various important religio-philosophical subjects of the great thinkers and writers of his and other religions. After a preliminary discussion of the nature and sources of knowledge he proceeds to prove the existence of God by showing that the world could not have existed from eternity and must have been created in time — creation implies a creator. This God is one and incorporeal and His unity and simplicity are not affected by the different aspects of His attributes. The division on Unity closes with a refutation of the prevailing opposing views, the dualists, infidels and Trinitarians. Free-will is the center of discussion of the second division, namely, of Justice. Psychology and ethics are, therefore, here taken up. In the whole work Islamic influence is evident. His purpose in writing this masterpiece was to defend Judaism and Jewish dogma. For example, in answer to the question of why investigate?[4] he answers — to know what we have from tradition; that we cannot do anything without tradition, and that the cause for people believing in false ideas is their laziness — their dulness. Saadia, as was stated above, covers the salient philosophical problems in his book. His sources are Jewish literature and tradition, the works of the Mutakallimûn, particularly the Mu'tazilites, and Aristotle, whose work on the "Categories" he knew at first hand.[5]

[3] The text used in this paper is the Hebrew translation of Judah ibn Tibbon of Saadia's work — the Yuzefov edition. I refer here to Prof. David Neumark's article on Saadia, in the "Hebrew Union College Annual," Vol. I, where, in addition to a review of Dr. Henry Malter's book on Saadia, he gives his own and original researches, pp. 503–573.

[4] See הקדמת המחבר, pp. 48–54.

[5] It should be stated here that the ten categories of Aristotle had influenced

His strong desire and purpose was to have people make a conscientious study of his book so that the readers may remove doubt and substitute therefor belief through knowledge for belief through tradition, and, more important, to be able through such study, to improve character and disposition which will affect man's life towards better thought and action, not only in his relationship with man but with God as well.[6]

2. *The Soul.*

Of the ten parts in Saadia's masterpiece, the sixth treats of the soul. Saadia, who was under the influence of Aristotle interpreted from the Neo-Platonic viewpoint, did not share in the Platonic conception of the dualism of matter and spirit, nor did he accept the tri-partite division of the soul. To him the soul is a spiritual substance which is created simultaneously with the body; it is a unit and finds its seat in the heart,[7] — heart and soul, therefore, being synonymous terms in the Bible. This soul — is indivisible and possesses a luminous nature like the spheres,[8] but, it is simpler, finer and purer than they, and has a unique characteristic in that it is endowed with thought. It was created by God out of the primal ether from which the angels were made, at the same time the body was made and

practically all the philosophers either directly or indirectly. These categories gave rise to the general classification of Substance and Accident — the latter being nine in number — quantity, quality, relation, place, time, position, possession, action, and passion. Saadia, in more than one way, employs this classification. For example, in order to show that God is not to be compared to any other thing in creation; God is the cause of all substance and accident, hence He is Himself neither the one or the other. See Part II, Chs. 9–12; pp. 95–102. Part VI, Ch. 1, p. 149.

[6] See pp. 38–39.

[7] P. 148: כי התחלת נפש האדם בלבו, עם שלמות צורת גופו. P. 154: ובענין אלה הכוחות טעה מי ששמה שני חלקים: אחד מהם בלב, והאחר בשאר הגוף, — אך השלשה לנפש אחת . . . ואחר כן התבאר לי כי משכנה בלב בני אדם, וכאשר הוא גלוי כי הגידים אשר נותנים לגוף החוש והתנועה צמיחתם כלם מן הלב. Note p. 94, Guttmann, J., on "Ab. ibn Daud" where he discusses this phase and also of Ibn Sina and others. See also Schmiedl, *l. c.*, notes, pp. 134 and 135.

[8] P. 152: ושצלמה צלם נקי כנקיות הגלגלים.

within the body. This union of body and soul was brought about in order to display that moral and ethical activity prescribed for it in the divine teaching. Should the *Soul* neglect this it would defile and contaminate its purpose and purity. Saadia follows up this discussion by saying that some substance adheres to the soul as does to the angels and thus accepts the Talmudic expressions with regard to abode of the soul after death. Saadia also combats the Hindu teaching of metempsychosis, which had been adopted by Plato and Pythagoras.[9]

The Study of Soul is nothing more, to Saadia, than a continuation of the study of God and His relationship to the rational part of His creation in the sublunar world. That man is endowed with a *soul* cannot be doubted, for, the activities of the soul of man are directly visible[10] — the problem which is difficult is that which deals with the *nature* of the soul. We have had in our previous discussions intimations of these various conceptions — Saadia enumerates them.[11] Some think the soul an accident of the body, others that it is a corporeal substance like air or fire, and still others, that there are several souls in man; these, Saadia refutes[12] and says that the *Soul* is too important in its functions to be an accident; it is not a corporeal substance because it has not their properties. As was said above, Saadia holds that the soul is indivisible, for if it did consist of two or more distinct parts, the perceptions of sense would not reach the reason and there would be no cooperation between these

[9] See p. 154, ch. 4, p. 160, ch. 8: ואקדם בתחלת מאמרי, כי הבורא יתברך, אשר ספרנו ענינו במה שקדם, מתכלית השקר שיאמר עליו שהוא מריע לאדם או שיעיל עליו, מפני שכל המקרים מסתלקים מעליו, ועוד כי פעליו כלם ישרים וטובים, ועוד כי לא ברא הבריאות כי אם להועילם, לא להזיקם אומר שאנשים ממי שנקראים יהודים, מצאתים אומרים בהשנות, וקוראים אותו ההעתקה, וענינו אצלם שרוח ראובן תשוב אל שמעון, ואחר כן בלוי, ואחר כן ביהודה, ויש מהם רבים שאומרים: יש פעמים שתהיה רוח האדם בבהמה ורוח הבהמה באדם, ודברים רבים מזה השגעון והערבוב. והסתכלתי במה שחושבים שהביאם אל המאמר הזה, ומצאתים ארבעה שבושים, וכול'.

[10] P. 149: אבל ראו פעלה.

[11] Pp. 149–150.

[12] P. 150: מצאתים כלם שקר מכמה צדדים . . . אבל נראה אותה [נפש] בענין הזה עצם שתהיה ראויה יותר מהפכים מקבולה. It is possible in this whole discussion that Israeli had much influence upon Saadia in re: differences and similarities. See Guttman, J., *l. c.*, pp. 3, 13, 40, 42, 44, 50, 1n3 64.

two powers.[13] Saadia, therefore, concludes that the Soul of man if a substance created by God at the time when the human body is completed — the soul is a substance and as pure as the celestial spheres[14] — it is rational. It uses the body as an instrument for its functions — when connected with the body the soul has three faculties, namely, reason, spirit, and desire[15] — all these three faculties reside in the heart, the source of sense and motion for the body. The soul purifies or defiles itself while it is in the body and man must strive to attain perfection.[16] Thus it is good for the Soul to be placed in the body.

3. *Reflective Analysis.*

In Saadia we have a great advance in the real interpretation of the nature of the soul. As was stated above, he leads to the discussion of the soul from a thorough analysis of God and his attributes. His premises, namely, that everything outside of God is created (therefore, creatio ex nihilo) and that there is no pure spirit outside of God, that all is composite, that it has matter, leads to the inevitable conclusion that God alone is immaterial.[17] His spirit manifests itself particularly in man;[18] the soul, which is created in man when the embryo is ready to

[13] P. 150, particularly the commentary שביל האמונה.

[14] P. 152, ch. 3.

[15] P. 153, ch. 6: וכאשר תתחבר [הנשמה] לגוף יראו לה ג' כחות: כח ההכרה, וכח הכעס, וכח התאוה. ועל־כן קראה אותה לשוננו (ב"ר פ"ג) בשלשה שמות: נפש, ורוח, ונשמה.

[16] See p. 155: ... כל שאלה שישאלו בה בני אדם בענין הנפש ראוי שאשיבנה אל זה השרש ואשיאנה עליו: ואומר, בעבור שהיתה בלתי פועלת לבדה בבניניה; התחייב חבורה אל דבר תגיע בו אל הפועל, ותגיע אל הנעם המתמיד, ואל ההצלחה הגמורה, כאשר בארנו במאמר החמישי. See also the commentary "שביל האמונה" *ad locum*, and Part V, Chs. 1–3, pp. 136–140.

[17] This is Aristotle's "Metaxsye" and parallel to Plato's "Theory of Ideas." In part I he gives all the prevailing theories and meets them all by asking — what is the *Motive* of Becoming? — and shows that they are against the principle of "Metaxsye."

[18] Note at the beginning of הקדמת המחבר (p. 36): ... ומצאו בה מוחשיהם מציאה ברורה וידעו בה ידיעותם ידיעת צדק ... ונצללו להם הראיות ... "They (i.e. men) found by it their sensual objects — a *clear finding*; as soon as the soul is put into them their faculties begin to function . . . with it proofs are clarified." — See also שביל האמונה thereto. See page 54 also.

receive it, exemplifies God's presence. God is incorporeal but nevertheless has wisdom, will and vitality — this is due to the all-prevailing spirit. Man, too, is impregnated with a form principle — the essence of which is not matter — but — mentality.[19] Saadia insists on חי (vitalism), יכול (voluntarism) and חכם (intellectualism)[20] as a unit and as constituting the essential attributes of God — our reasoning faculty arrives at these concepts with one act of thinking — they are all included in the word *Maker*. With regard to the soul — I choose to appropriate these concepts insofar that since the *Soul* is created at the same time with the body it is the Maker of that unit — personality. Its process of development is in the order given (in note 20). The mental phase is the all-important part although the other two חי and יכול are necessary in the whole arrangement.[21]

Following the discussion of the above — we may emphasize here, as another contribution of Saadia's, the concept of "ectoplasm"[22] — the soul *is* this and the soul gets its impetus at the time the embryo is ready to receive it — this ectoplasm[23] may also be called the motivating force in the process of the Soul's realization from potentiality to actuality.[24] This ectoplasm is created and is not, like Aristotle's "ether," eternal, — however — this dynamic power has, from my own reflection on the matter, the unique characteristic of making the *soul* attain immortality.[25]

[19] In re: Prophecy, Ethical laws and Revelation, Saadia emphasizes Reason as the first source of Revelation and of Law. In this he anticipates Kant. See Part III, Chap. 10, p. 122; Part V, Ch. 8, p. 147; Part VII, Ch. 2, page 165.

[20] Part II, ch. 1, p. 87, etc., particularly, ch. 4 — p. 91 and commentary: ואחר כן אומר שמצאתי מדרך העיון מה־שיורה שהוא חי יכול חכם הוא מה שהתאמת לנו שהוא ברא הדברים ובכח שכלנו התברר כי לא יעשה כי־אם יכול ולא יוכל כי־אם חי ולא היה העשוי המתוקן אלא ממי שידע קודם שיעשה ואיך יהיה.

[21] George Santayana in his essay on "Privacy" says "life is to be won and not snatched" — true, here it is intimated that life to be *made* — to be created.

[22] A term used by Dr. David Neumark which expresses most admirably the creative factor in soul development. I may say here that body and germ-plasm alone do not develop a soul — it takes an energizing force — this "*metaxsye*" of Saadia to start the process of development.

[23] Cf. Aristotle's "ether."

[24] Cf. Israeli's view.

[25] The scope of this book precludes a discussion on immortality — I may

— It does approximate the divine — in its original essence[26] — for it has in its incipiency a divine element[27] which can increase in vitality, in power and in intelligence. I concur in this reflective analysis with Saadia, and say that conduct does play an important part in the development of the soul. Conduct is the tool, so to speak, that can make a person use or abuse[28] the inherent capabilities and possibilities within the Soul. "The still small voice" within man may be a true guide for the Soul's course. This immanence of God within us, given to us at birth, may lead us to a complete harmonious arrangement of the desires of our complex nature.[29] This would be conducive towards a greater perfection of conduct and morals. — Again, it is *Wisdom* that is the controlling and directing influence in our conduct so that the Soul may be developed from a state of dormancy to activity and appropriation of the divine.

only state here my view on the matter. I appreciate Saadia's presentation of the world to come which follows logically from his discussion on ectoplasm.

[26] See p. 152, Ch. 3: ושעצמה עצם נקי כנקיות הגלגלים.

[27] I may call this a parallel to Israeli's "spark" that emanates from the original splendor.

[28] Part V, Chs. 1–3, pp. 136–140.

[29] See Part X, pp. 197–215. This chapter may be considered as an appendix to Saadia's work. — Written, as it was as an afterthought, in order to give a psychological basis for human conduct.

V.

BACHYA BEN JOSEPH IBN PAKUDA

1. *Life and Works.*

Very little is known of the life of Bachya. He lived in Spain and had the office of "Dayan" or judge of his community. It is questionable whether he lived after or before Gabirol and, in the case of the former, many say he is indebted to Gabirol for many of his views on philosophy and ethics. There are, however, many convincing data to the effect that Bachya lived previous to Gabirol.[1] However, we here need not be concerned with these intricate historical problems.[2] We do not know his exact dates; we do know that he was a highly respected man in his day, profoundly religious and liberal-minded.

Bachya's contribution is in the fact that before him there was not written a systematic book on Ethics.[3] His book and his masterpiece is called "חובות הלבבות" — the "Duties of the Hearts" — dealing with the duties of Heart and Mind. It was originally written in Arabic and translated into Hebrew by the Tibbons and was destined to become one of the most popular as well as the most authoritative expositions of spiritual Judaism.[4] The name of the book implies a Mohammedan influence for they, as well as Bachya, distinguished between outward

[1] See Neumark, *loc. cit.*, pp. 485–493.

[2] For a good and brief account of the theology of Bachya, see Kaufmann, David, in "Gesammelte Schriften," 1910.

[3] Of course, the Bible, Talmud and Midrashim, the "Sayings of the Fathers," Gabirol's "choicest of the Pearls," etc., etc., all have ethical content — but there did not exist a treatise giving a scientific working out of a system of ethics based on one central thought and claiming universal validity as Bachya's does.

[4] The other works of Bachya include a "Poem on Unity;" a "Prayer" and "Barechi Nafshi."

ceremonial or observance, known as "visible wisdom" and "duties of the limbs" and inward intention and feeling called "hidden wisdom" and "duties of the hearts."[5] By the "duties of the heart" Bachya understands the *whole* of conduct and of thought as its ideal essence. To him the outward ritual act is, morally considered, of no importance, except insofar as it represents a manifestation of character and an expression of intention. The "duties" are rational and like precepts they are both positive and negative.[6] All these duties of the heart are not visible to others and God alone can judge whether one's feelings and motives are pure or not. Reason, law and tradition are the sources of knowledge.

The religious philosophy of Bachya is eclectic. The central point of his whole theology is the conception of the unity of God. He is Neo-Platonic in that he accepts matter, as a principle of evil, and the theory of ideas.[7]

His Book contains ten chapters, or "Gates": the first five may be considered the theoretical discussion, and the last five the practical. The attributes, unity, service of God and confidence in God are minutely analyzed; humility, conscience, repentance, temperance and love of God are also Gates, through all of which, man may pierce the gloom of this earth and enter into true communion with God. It is the duty of man to enter through these gates. Throughout his treatise he insists upon inward purification — this the previous writers have not stressed according to Bachya[8] and to this task he desires to purify religion itself from within with an emphasis upon the necessity of our thoughts and words being sincere and constant in the service of God. This service of God comes through a unity of heart and intellect — the latter must reason out the undeniable truth that

[5] The latest authority on Bachya is Yahuda, who edited the Arabic text of Bachya's work under the tile "Al Hidaya 'Ila Faraid Al-Qulub des Bachya ibn Joseph ibn Paquda," Leyden, 1912.

[6] See Kaufmann, *loc. cit.*, pp. 3–20, for a clear exposition of the various sources of Bachya's work.

[7] Kaufmann, *loc. cit.*, pp. 20–25.

[8] See "Duties of the Heart," Warsaw edition, 1875, הקדמה, pp. 9–28, and Kaufmann, *loc. cit.* ,pp. 4–5.

God is a *unit.* One and Inseparable, and, the former, the heart, must feel it and make the person speak it.[9]

2. *The Soul.*

The limits set to our thesis preclude going much further into the many philosophic — ethical discussions of Bachya; we must turn our attention to the subject of the development of the soul. Surely — it is, with Bachya, an all-embracing and an all-important topic. As was intimated above Bachya implies, by the expression "Duties of the Heart," the whole of human conduct and thought, embracing therein, the conception of *thought*, particularly, in its ideal essence. The כונה — intention, the heart, the inside (תוכו) must be like the outside (כברו). The whole of conduct as such belongs to the domain of ethics. The things done and said are either wrong or right in accordance with the intention with which it is done or left undone.[10] Our intentions are conditioned to a great measure by our state of mind and feeling — this being so, it is, therefore, incumbent upon us to perfect our souls, as this is the foundation of Ethics. Bachya insists that we are to *live* our lives and the injunction he gives is not "do this or that" but "be this." The perfection of the soul can only be brought about by the conscientious effort on the part of the individual to become "at one" with God — to love Him and to serve Him —[11] to study about nature and thus praise and love His works and thus know Him — know His goodness and wisdom as exhibited in nature. — A knowledge such as this, of nature and God, leads to reverence for and trust in Him. This leads to an important condition in man's *soul* — it gives a purity and sincerity uninfluenced by the passive values of his day — He centers all his intentions and thoughts and actions towards one end — namely — towards a love of God — the Soul soars up and on towards this communion with Him — founded — necessarily, upon a "unity of conduct."[12]

[9] See gate I, ch. 1: על־כן אמרתי בגדר היחוד השלם שהוא השוואת הלב והלשון ביחוד הבורא אחר שידע להביא ראיה עליו ולדעת אופני אמתת אחדותו מדרך העיון.

[10] Cf. Halevi's expression thereto.

[11] Gate V, pp. 3–35.

[12] See Gate V, p. 3, etc.: ... כל מעשי העבודה מיוחדים לאלהים ...

The chapter which is mostly pertinent to our direct inquiry is that of self-examination which follows immediately those of humility and repentance. — To Bachya, this appraisement of one's self is conducive to an inner-wholesomeness towards a greater humility and a more thorough desire for repentance. It is a cleansing process for the soul. Reflection is most essential; — reflection upon God, His unity, wisdom and goodness. — Thus the soul becomes an *active* part in one's life. The Soul stimulates the mind and increases the spiritual resources. The soul becomes enriched and yearns for a continued progress in its struggle for perfectibility.[13] What is meant by חשבון הנפש; whether this is alike in all men; in what divers manner is this חשבון הנפש conducted by men; of what benefit is this self-examination; is it obligatory for man to continually go through this process or not and, lastly, in what way is man obligated to connect his deed with self-examination. The answers have all been intimated above. The result of positive answers to the above surely could not but lead to a pious individual and a pure soul.[14] Through this self-examination one can readily see that the soul increases in strength and is able to control his body.[15] As an outcome of such conscientious self-examination one practices many virtues[16] — temperance (פרישות) to Bachya (as to Maimuni) is all-important and, man, through this path, this gate, attains his goal — namely, purification of the soul, and making it like the angels. This brings man to the highest stage of development — his soul is cleansed — purified — through self-purification to the central

[13] Gate VIII, pp. 82–126. See particularly the commentary "מרפא נפש" following on p. 82: ... והיה החשבון עם הנפש אחד מתנאיה ...

[14] See a most forcible advocacy of such life by Henry Dwight Sedgwick in his "Pro Vita Monastica." In this he takes modern life to task and urges a return to a sane "monasticism" — giving us a "serenity of spirit upon which depends our power to see truth, to do justice and to think no evil."

[15] Note particularly Bachya's premise in Ch. II of Gate VII on תשובה, p. 62: והחלק השני השב בלבו ובאבריו ועומד בשכלו כנגד יצרו ומתנהג להכריח נפשו ולהלחם עם תאוותיה עד שינצחנה וימנענה ממה שישנאהו הבורא ית'.

[16] Bachya evidently was influenced by the Greek classification of the four cardinal virtues — wisdom, courage, temperance and justice. Truly, we may say that they are as much Hebrew as they are Greek (with which I concur) but Bachya's sources as we have seen were truly Jewish.

and controlling principle. Man — has reached a high spirituality — a true love for and communion with God.

3. *Reflective Analysis.*

There are two outstanding points that I wish, herewith, to emphasize in order to focus our discussion — namely — Bachya's world view and his emphasis upon reason. These two ideas are pertinent to our topic of soul-development and of importance to our discussion of the individual aspect of the soul.

Conduct — in all its ramifications, is the all-pervading emphasis of Bachya. The right conduct is the right path, the true gate to the higher world of the spirit. All the yearnings and impulses to virtuous actions on the part of man spring from the point of contact between the human soul and the yet-to-be-seen soul of the universe. The individual with a "live and palpitating" heart, with a conscience at rest, who is in communion with God and is appreciative and grateful to Him for all His bounties, it is this individual who is able to recognize the obligations of ethical conduct. Such developments of a soul come not from the outer circle and environment of sociological duties to the inner and smaller social group — the family — to the individual soul;[17] not from the circumference and the matrix of complex deeds and activities to the center of ideals and soul perfection — but — from the *center*, the active and *creative soul* to the outward act. With such world view — one can readily see that it is conducive towards activity, creativity and accomplishment. The individual is given the soul and this soul[18] is in constant conflict with all the passions of the body in order to cleanse itself from materiality and corporeality so that it may be in "love with God."[19] It is because Bachya

[17] Contra Greek idea.

[18] Gate X, p. 152, and Kaufmann, *loc. cit.* (and notes), p. 86.

[19] This "love of God" and the nature of the soul he explains as follows: Gate X, Ch. I, p. 152: אבל מה ענין האהבה באלהים, הוא כלות הנפש ונטותה בעצמה אל הבורא, כדי שתדבק באורו העליון. והוא שהנפש עצם פשוט רוחני, נוטה אל הדומה לה מהאישים הרוחניים, ומתרחקת בטבעתה מאשר הוא כנגדה מן הגופות העבות. See also Kaufmann, pp. 86–87 and note in re: Gazzali.

realizes that man is full of sense-complexes, so to speak, that he exhorts man to overcome his dual nature.[20] Man is made up of body and soul (limbs and heart) and both alike are given through the grace and kindness of God: the one is visible and the other invisible; our duties and worship therefore, are two-fold, activity on the part of man in righteous conduct and secondly the invisible activity of the heart and mind. To acknowledge the Unity of God immediately places our soul in action and in an attitude of reverence and love for Him. Our senses[21] unite and co-operate, our mind becomes active and the soul becomes a unifying factor and agent for our senses — bringing us ever closer and closer to God.[22]

Bachya places great emphasis upon reason as the great help-mate of the *soul* in its effort toward perfection. Reason must control the desires and passions of man[23]; — with reason properly functioning man does rise towards a greater self-control and a resultant purer soul — the eyes of the soul begin to see part of the invisible universal soul.[24] The love of God and the fear of God will then be his, through which means, his soul tears itself away from earthly affairs[25] and desires, and, it becomes part of God. — The darkness becomes light and the invisible becomes visible.

[20] In this connection, see Gate III. pages 178–197, and Kaufmann, *loc. cit.*, pp. 6–7 and interesting note thereto.

[21] Gate I, p. 88 and Kaufmann, pp. 12–13 and note: וממה שצריך שתדע ויתבאר אצלך מענין החושים הגשמים אשר זכרנו, והחושים הנפשיים אשר הם הזכרון והמחשבה והרעיון והזמם וההכרה, שכולם מגיעים עד ענין אחד, והוא השכל הנותן להם כח להשגת הענינים, ולכל חוש מהם ענין מיוחד להשיג מוחשו לא יושג בזולתו.

[28] Bachya's ecstasy is comparable to that of Gabirol — see Gate X, pp. 163–8.

[23] See Gate VIII, ch. 6, and Gate III, pp. 150–2.

[24] See Gate VIII, ch. 5, cf. Gabirol.

[25] Gate X, p. 152.

VI.

SOLOMON IBN GABIROL — 1021–1058 (1070)

1. *Life and Works.*

The scene of Jewish intellectual activity in the eleventh century shifts, for various reasons, from the East to the West. The schools closed with the death of Saadia. — Mohammedan influence prevailed in Spain with favor and grace to the Jews. The exodus from Babylonia found a splendid haven in Spain wherein was destined to spring forth some of the greatest Jewish writers for the following five centuries. Gabirol is the first Jewish philosopher in Spain. He is, of course, better known as and celebrated for his synagogal poetry, for these were and are always extant in the various Jewish communities. It took quite a long while before his philosophical work — entitled "מקור חיים" (or the Latin "Fons Vitae")[1] was known — and — fully attributed to him. This was primarily due to the fact that it was originally written in Arabic — and — its style was not conducive towards elaboration or easy translation. It remained for the commentator and critic Shem Tob Folaquera (1225–1290) to be the first to translate Gabirol's מקור חיים into Hebrew — and this only in the salient parts of his work. There was a Latin translation about a century before this of Folaquera's, and this was done at the instigation of the Christian Clericals; — this was a good translation and was not overlooked as was that of Folaquera. Gabirol's Jewish identity was not known, his name being Avicebron[2] — and he was at different times taken now as a Mohammedan and then as a Christian. Gabirol nowhere, in this "Fons Vitae,"

[1] I shall only treat of this work in this paper. His other work תיקון מדות הנפש "Improvement of the Qualities of the Soul" (which is parallel to Bachya's) is Gabirol's ethics. Its thesis is that knowledge and practice brings a higher life to the soul. He is, in this, greatly influenced by Aristotle, Galen and Hippocrates and like Israeli, but more elaborately, classifies the virtues of man in accordance with the senses.

[2] Also, Avencebrol and Avicembron.

shows his Jewish heritage. The treatise is purely a speculative treatise and nowheres does he try to reconcile his philosophic views with his religious faith. For these reasons Gabirol was, for a long time, never spoken of as a Jewish philosopher, though, under the name of Avicebron, he was quoted, defended and attacked by Scholastic writers.

It is important in this connection to note that his thesis, namely, that there is a universal matter underlying all existence outside of God, was the cause for the formation of two strong schools in the Christian church. Firstly, the Dominicans, led by Thomas Aquinas, who opposed this un-Aristotelian principle, and, secondly, the Franciscans with Duns Scotus as their leader, accepting this thesis of Gabirol.[3]

Gabirol is Neo-Platonic and, he also adopted many Aristotelian principles and conceptions; matter and form, potentiality and actuality, the categories, the theory of ideas, and the classifications of the principles of the soul were part of his philosophical speculations, as they were, to a greater or lesser degree, of the many thinkers of his and later times. To Gabirol, matter is the underlying substance for all being from the highest to the lowest with one exception and that is God.[4] The theory of emanation

[3] See Munk, *Melanges de Philosophie Juive et Arabe*, Paris, 1859, p. 291 ff.; Guttmann, *Die Scholastik des Dreizehnten Jahrhunderts*, Breslau, 1920, pp. 60–85; *id.*, *Die Philosophie des Salomon ibn Gabirol*, Gottingen, 1889, p. 54 ff., and p. 1 ff. for list of other works of Gabirol. As to other works pertaining to Gabirol we may mention:

a) Jourdain, *Recherches Critiques sur l'age et l'origine des traductions Latines l'Aristote*. 2nd Ed. Paris, 1843, p. 197, note.
b) Kaufmann, *Studien über Solomon ibn Gabirol*, Budapest, 1899.
c) Baeumker, Clemens, Latin translation in the *Beitrage zur Geschichte der Philosophie des Mittelalters*, Vol. I, pts. 2–4.
d) *Id.*, *Avencebrolis Fons Vitae*, Munster, 1892–95, Prolegomena.
e) Seyerlen in *Theologische Jahrbücher*, edited by Zeller XV and XVI.

It may here be noted that the fundamental and basic sentence underlying Gabirol's whole philosophy is כל עצם זולתי האל הוא מורכב מחומר וצורה — contra Th. Aquinas in Quaest. disputt., quest. de anima, art. VI).

[4] It is well here to go to the original sources and read Hebrew (and Latin and French translations with notes. See Munk and Baeumker, *loc. cit.*), pp. 120–121; p. 313. See Falaquera's (in Munk's *loc. cit.*) מקור חיים, Ch. V, Pp. 40–41, two very important passages:

does play an important part in Gabirol's philosophy — in fact — it is adopted as a whole just as his predecessors did. His philosophy of the worlds depend upon it. Thus, matter emanates from the creator and forms the basis of all emanations that are to follow — matter underlies form and this principle is the guiding one in the four worlds. The spiritual substances of the celestial world, have matter underlying their form — Matter itself — is spiritual or intelligible and not corporeal.[5] To Gabirol corporeality and materiality are two different things. Prime matter, as it emanates from the creator, invests all and assumes various gradations, the further this gets away from its original source, the creator, the less spiritual it becomes, and it assumes corporeality. The universe to Gabirol (like to Plotinus and the Kabbalistic writers) is a graded process of cosmic existences or worlds with God at one end and the corporeal world at the other — and in between them are the spiritual substances, Intelligence, Soul and Nature.[6] This is the world picture of Gabirol and within the limits indicated he places man and gives him a non-corporeal cause as a motivating power for proper functioning.

P. 40: ואני אתן לך כלל קצר תסמוך עליו בציור (זה) עמוד בשכלך אצל נדר הבריאה ארצה למד התחלת האחדות היסוד בצורת וציר [עצם] אין לו ראשית ולא אחרית והוא עצם הבורא ית׳ וצייר כל־הנמצא הרוחני והגשמי קס־בו כציורך ענין מהענינים קם בנפש כי אז [תראה] כי כח הבורא ית׳ וית׳ (בכל) נמצא (וכן תראה כח העליון מהנמצא ועצמו) בתחתון ממנו אל התכלה התחתונה והוא גדר ההפסק ואז תצייר המשך היסוד והצורה מהעליון אל התחתון המשך אחד.

P. 41: והיסוד קים בידיעת האלוה ית׳ כקיום הארץ באמצע השמים והצורה מזהרת עליו שוקעת בו כזהר אור השמש על האויר והארץ ושקיעתו בהם ונקראת זאת הצורה אור מאחר שהיתה האמרה אשר ממנה שפעה הצורה אור כלומר אור שכלי לא אור חושי ועוד כי מדרך האור לגלות צורת הדבר ולהראותה אחר היותה נעלמת וכן הצורה כשתדבק ביסוד יראה בה הדבר אחר היותו נעלם והיה בה נמצא.

[5] In this connection, see the following: Baeumker, *loc. cit.*, pp. 333–335; Falaquera, V, Ps. 67–69. Baeumker, *loc. cit.*, pp. 229–230; Falaquera, IV, P. 1. Baeumker, *loc. cit.*, p. 296; Falaquera, , V, P. 27. This last reference is both important and interesting and is well quoting here — and for future considerations: והראיה כי הצורות הרוחניות נעלמות בצורות הגשמיות היא כי הנפש תחנה הגוף בכחותיה וידבק כל מה מכחותיה בצורה הנאותה לה בדקיקות כי היא תפרק צורת האיכות והכמות מצורת העצם ואחר כך תפרק צורת העצם וצורת הטבע וצורת הטבע מצורת הנפש וצורת הנפש מצורת השכל וצורת השכל מהיסוד הראשון וצריך שתדע כי מי שהיטיב לדעת פרוק אלו הצורות והכיר כל אחד מאלו העצמים מהאחר הגיע לתכלית הידיעה והתענוג.

[6] See Baeumker, *loc. cit.*, p. 196; Falaquera, *loc. cit.*, III, P. 10.

2. *The Soul.*

As with other philosophers Gabirol adopts the tri-partite classification of the Soul. Man is microcosm in his world-scheme, and he partakes of the intermediate worlds and of the corporeal world. Man's body consists of the lowest matter and therefore is typical of the corporeal world.[7] The body is at rest and needs an agent to hold it together and to make it act. This, Gabirol calls Nature — The body needs to function properly — it needs a non-corporeal cause — this is the *soul*, in its vegetative, animalistic and rationalistic functions. When man passes through these stages he is ready to accomplish the highest stage — that is perfection — when he has apprehended the intelligence, when he attains that stage of immediate intellectual intuition — the possession of the forms of things known — that is true knowledge. Gabirol draws analogy between the microcosm of man and the universe and there are corresponding cosmic existences, principles and powers. Thus there is a cosmic Intelligence, a cosmic soul[8] and a cosmic nature, the three emanating in the order given, from the prime source.[9] This is in short Gabirol's discussion on soul. He, however, gives us some strong points insofar as our thesis is concerned; namely, the idea of soul-development. This point we are now ready to take up.

3. *Reflective Analysis.*

Looking over Gabirol's world-scheme we find that his concept of *universal matter* is of great aid to us in our researches upon the topic of creativity. As was stated above, he distinguishes between matter and corporeality. He adjures man to lessen the latter and appropriate more and more of the former — the prime matter. It is within man's power to get out of corpore-

[7] Baeumker, p. 208; Falaquera, III, p. 44, particularly the closing sentence: ואני חושב כי הנהגת הפרטית נמשכת אחר הנהגת העולם הכללי וזו היא הדרך להגיע אל ההצלחה השלמה והשגת התענוג האמתי שהוא כונתנו.

[8] Embracing the three divisions enumerated.

[9] Munk, *loc. cit.*, p. 64, note 1, emphasizes the individual aspect: this I shall elaborate later.

ality.[10] The Soul, with its faculties, takes hold of the body; it "encamps" within the body. The essence and the power of the lower substances are latent[11] within each individual and can be aroused to action — the lower substances have emanated from the higher and more perfect and simpler substance and can attain this increased perfection.[12]

I choose to tread on dangerous ground when I herewith desire to appropriate Gabirol's principle of matter and form as pervading even the spiritual substance.[13] The "differential," (if I may use this mathematical term) between two things, between two persons, if you please, is not the *matter* but the *form*. This holds true of the intelligible substances, Intelligence and soul — which are alike in their substantiality but are different in their *form*.[14] It is here that we find a true element of creativity. Each individual can create within himself a unique, a distinct "differential," giving him a "form principle" through which he can appropriate a greater part of the Intelligence, a greater part of the universal matter and of the Universal form. I do not desire to lessen the individual emphasis[15] — or have him absorbed in the universalism as expressed. The individual effort, exertion, and the degree of appropriation of the universal does not sublimate the individual in the cosmic whole.[16] The individual man in this process of obtaining pure *form* attains a complete identity with the ultimate,[17] with a more comprehen-

[10] See full quotation above from Falaquera, V, p. 27: כי הנפש תחנה הגוף בכחותיה.

[11] Contra Saadia, who holds that these are created.

[12] See Falaquera, V, 19. Baeumker, p. 175; Falaquera, III, P. 27, and Munk's notes thereto.

[13] A very enlightening essay correlative to this point is that of Prof. W. H. Sheldon, "Soul and Matter," in the *Philosophical Review*, March, 1922.

[14] Baeumker, *loc. cit.*, pp. 211, 213, 217–218; Falaquera (and notes) IV Pp. 1–4.

[15] See Falaquera III, 44 and Munk's note thereto: also III, 3, where this significant statement is made: והנפש נבדלת לגוף ולולז הרוח האמצעי ביניהם לא היה דבק אחד מהם באחר.

[16] See Munk's note to Falaquera's, IV, p. 3.

[17] Baeumker, *loc. cit.*, pp. 258, 268, 322. Falaquera V, p. 55 — particularly note the following: . . . ומי שנפשו דקה ושכלו זך עד שיהיה [אפשר] לו לפלש בהם וההכנסה מהם כבר הגיע אל התכלית והגיע אל התכלה והיה רוחני אלהי מתענג בקרוב מהטוב השלם והעמוד תנועתו ויתמיד תענוגו.

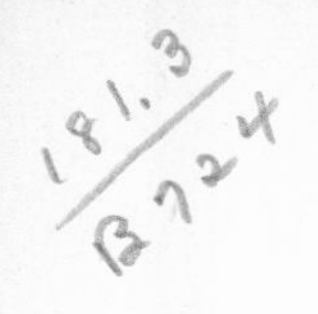

sive reality and this results in an enervating situation that is a stimulant to further action and choice.

The discussion of matter and form gives me another thought of importance, insofar as it relates to the development of soul. We see from the above that matter has no real existence without form — both come from God — matter from His *essence* and form from His attribute (Wisdom, Word, or Will).[18] The Will of God is that which works upon matter. It is in this we find a parallel to the Aristotelian conception of Soul — that it is the function of the body — of matter — it moulds matter. The soul of man, in its development, can become creative and dynamic and insofar as it does so it approximates and patterns itself after the Will of God.

The last, and very important, point I wish to stress is the emphasis upon the active intellect — the שכל הפועל so much in use by most of the philosophers. Gabirol stresses this and insists that man, for his own benefit, should use this active intellect so that his soul may fully function and appropriate the world of Spirit, the world of Intelligence. The Soul should, through the active intellect, make man tear himself away more and more from corporeality so that this corporeal world should seem as though it is floating in the spiritual substances as a small boat in the sea and as a bird in the air.[19] This active intellect, when it is made to function, does make the soul to soar into realms still untrodden; should not the prospect of this journey stimulate individuals to attempt such attainment? It is a hard task, but, truly creative and permanent. The essence of the true intelligence can thus be viewed and God truly becomes part of the individual.[20] He emerges out from the corporeal world and unites with the upper world wherein the soul properly belongs.[21]

[18] Baeumker, p. 306; Falaquera, V, P. 34. (והצורה) . . . תצא מהכח אל הפעל בלא זמן ועל־כן לא תמצא כהרף עין ריקה מן היסוד ואין בצורה היוצאה מן הנפש כן And Baeumker, p. 326; Falaquera, V, P. 60.

[19] Baeumker, p. 204; and Falaquera, III, P. 37. ותראה העולם הגשמי . . . בכללו ישוט בהם כאלו הוא ספינה בים או עוף באויר.

[20] Falaquera, V, p. 25, and see note of Munk, p. 106: ועל כן אמרו . . . החכמים כי אין הגון בענין הצורה האמתית זולתי השכל הראשון והוא הנקרא אצלם השכל הפועל.

[21] Baeumker, p. 4; Falaquera I, P. 2.

VII.

JOSEPH IBN ZADDIK — (d. 1149)

1. *Life and Works.*

Joseph Ben Jacob ibn Zaddik was a Rabbi, poet and philosopher. Little is known of his life though record exists that, because of the fact that he was a Talmudist of high repute, he was appointed in 1138 "Dayyan," or Judge, of the Jewish community at Cordova, in Spain. This office he held jointly with Maimon, the father of Maimonides, until he died in 1149. Ibn Zaddik was also a gifted poet and several of his poems are found in the Sephardic and African "Machzorim."[1] Important as was the Rabbinical knowledge of ibn Zaddik, as was also his poetic achievement, still his fame rests mostly upon his activity as a religious philosopher. Ibn Zaddik wrote a short treatise in Arabic[2] which was translated into Hebrew under the title, "Olam Katon," or "Microcosm." Maimonides knew Joseph ibn Zaddik and speaks favorably of him in a letter to Samuel ibn Tibbon, the noted translator, where he said his tendency is like that of the "Brothers of Purity"[3] — an indication that ibn Zaddik was a Neo-Platonist, combining Aristotelian physics with

[1] See Kaempf, Saul Isaak, *Nichtandalusische Poesie andalusischer Dichter* Prag, 1858, I, p. 13: — quotation from *Al-Harizi*:

> "Wenn R. Josef ben Zaddik seinen Dichtergeist lasst walten,
> dann muss der Wissens Meer sich spalten."

A poem addressed to Judah Halevi, about his visit to Cordova en route to Palestine, is included in the collection of Halevi's poems.

[2] The Arabic title is "Al-'Alam al-Saghir" — which was translated (according to Steinschneider) by Nalvim ha-Ma'arabi into Hebrew. I have used the Hebrew text as per Horovitz, without corrections. See his volume regarding same, especially pp. XIII–XIX.

[3] Letters to Maimonides ("Iggeroth"), Amsterdam, 1712, p. 146: ואמנם ספר העולם הקטן שבחר רבי יוסף לא ראיתיו, אבל אני ידעתי את האיש ואת שיחו, והכרתי ערך מעלתו ומעלת ספרו, כי בלא ספק הנהיג בו מנהג בעלי התארים.

Platonic and Plotinian metaphysics, ethics and psychology.[4] This is evident upon a careful perusal of ibn Zaddik's philosophical work, especially in his discussions on the nature of God's attributes, of the divine will, and of the nature of evil. A study of the book of ibn Zaddik's shows a manifest decrease of the theories of the Kalam and a decided antipathy to the Karaite leader and representative Joseph al Basir.[5] He was an eclectic and was greatly influenced by Saadia, Bachya, Pseudo-Bachya, and, especially by Gabirol, although differing with Gabirol in many theories, among them Gabirol's theory of emanation and his mysticism of a Neo-Platonic nature. Ibn Zaddik used secondary sources, and, particularly is this seen in the free use he makes of Aristotle — the use of a definition.[6] Ibn Zaddik did not limit himself to any specific philosophy or metaphysics; his treatise is more of a compendium of science, philosophy, and theology in Jewish literature: the small book is for beginners, who get therefrom a summary view of the world and of the unique place of man in the world, so that he may fulfill his purpose in the world. In this plan of treatment, we find how great an influence the "Brethren of Purity" had upon him.

The treatise, "Olam Katon," comprises four main divisions, with sections to each.[7] Ibn Zaddik begins with the exhortation that the highest duty of man is to acquire the elementary and

[4] The books referred to in this chapter of specific nature are: Horovitz, S., *Der Mikrokosmos des Josef ibn Saddik*, Breslau, 1903, including the Hebrew text to be referred to in this chapter, and, Doctor, Max, *Die Philosophie des Josef (ibn) Zaddik*, Münster, 1895. Both books give detailed account of the sources of the many views expressed by ibn Zaddik.

[5] See Franke, *Ein Mu'tazilitischer Kalam aus dem 10ten Jahrhundert*, Wien, 1872. For a thorough discussion of the sources of ibn Zaddik with textual references, see Horovitz, *loc. cit.*, pp. III–X.

[6] Note the discussion of "Soul" in the following pages — in re Aristotle's discussion of "Soul" in "de Anima."

[7] The divisions are as follows (Text p. 2):

המאמר הראשון — בהקדמות והצעות יצטרך אליהם להבא ובמיני העולם הזה, וכשהוא חולף אין לו עמידה.

המאמר השני — בידיעת האדם עצמו, ושהוא עולם קטן, ומה הענין אשר בשבילו קראוהו הפילוסופים עולם קטן.

המאמר השלישי — בעיקרים וכללים מחכמת האלהות.

המאמר הרביעי — בביאור כללים מן מעשים טובים ומעבירות, והגמול והעונש ואמתתם.

primary principles of the knowledge of God, and, that, through this knowledge, the human soul builds up its conception of things. Ibn Zaddik then proceeds to treat of matter and form, of substance and accident, and, of the various compositions of the parts of the world. This first division concludes with the central idea which prompted the writing of the book, namely, the comparison between the outer world (macrocosm) and man (microcosm).[8] Ibn Zaddik endeavors, in his book, to give the meanings of such terms as "perfection" and "permanent good." Man rises continually in equal gradations and concomitantly with the true knowledge of himself. The corporeal world is represented by his body and the spiritual world by his rational soul: Man attains the highest field of learning, namely, philosophy, the science of sciences and the end thereof, for, it is the means whereby he attains the true knowledge of the Creator.[9]

Ibn Zaddik proceeds to discuss the process of knowing. Man perceives in two ways — through sense and through intellect, the former giving him the accidents of things: reason alone can pierce through to the essence of an object — and thus alone can man attain the knowledge of the universal. The body of man (sense) which is gross can only know the surface (particulars) of things while the spirit, the intellect, the soul, is fine and penetrating. The knowledge in the world may be, according to ibn Zaddik, classified as necessary (or immediate) and demonstrated (or mediate);[10] the former, necessary knowledge, is that which no sane person can deny: this may come to us from the data of sense or the reason. The knowledge, however, coming to us through the reason is superior to that coming to us through the senses, and man alone is capable of attaining this knowledge.

[8] Cf. Plato's "Timaeus," 47b and the "Brethren of Purity."

[9] Pages 1–2 of Hebrew text, Horovitz, *loc. cit.*, ושמתי כוונתי לבאר ידיעת האדם אמתת עצמו, לפי שמידיעתו לעצמו ידע הכל, ומי שידע עצמו אפשר שידע זולתו, ומי שלא ידע את עצמו כ"ש שלא ידע זולתו. ועל־כן נקרא האדם עולם קטן, לפי שיש בו דמות מכל מה שבעולם גופו כמעלת העולם הגשמי ונפשו החכמה כמעלת העולם הרוחני. ובענין זה אמרו הפילוסופים בשומם חק ורשם לפילוסופיא, כי הפילוסופיא היא ידיעת האדם נפשו, כי מידיעת נפשו ידע הכל, ר"ל עולם הגשמות ועולם הרוחני. וזאת היא חכמת הפילוסופיא שהיא חכמת החכמות.

[10] Cf. Royce, Josiah, *The World and the Individual*, where this is fully discussed.

Demonstrated, or, mediate knowledge, is based upon necessary knowledge and is attained through the process of logical inference.[11] Ibn Zaddik then discusses the corporeal world and premises the discussion by saying that matter is the foundation and principle of a thing — and that all natural and artificial things have matter and form.[12] This holds true also of spiritual things, for, in such things the genus is its matter and the species is form, its specific difference is comparable to the efficient cause, and the individual to the final cause. In reality there is no matter without form, but, in thought, we can remove the form and leave the matter. Ibn Zaddik does focus consideration when he discusses substance and describes it as that which bears opposite and changing qualities: matter, receiving form is substance — and — absolute substance is simple and spiritual, for we can perceive it through the five senses. This is comparable to Gabirol when he discusses substance as supporting the ten categories.

Ibn Zaddik discusses the corporeal world and its relation to the celestial spheres, the elements, and motion; he concludes that the sphere moves in a circle, the most perfect of all motions, having neither beginning nor end: it is more perfect than all bodies — and the knowledge of God which is hidden from us is not hidden from it. With the four elements in the sublunar world we have generation and decay, which continuous process is proof that this world is not permanent, for change is the basis of its processes.[13] Man, also, is subject to generation and decay,

[11] Text pp. 3–6. דע, יחנך הבורא, כי האדם ישיג המושגות בשני ענינים: האחד בהרגש והאחד בשכל . . . כי מדע ההרגש אינו כי אם באישים כלומר: לא ישיג בהרגש הכללית כאשר ישיגם בנפש, שהנפש תשיג המינים הגבוהים והמינים השפלים. וידיעת הנפש היא אמת הדברים וטבעם שהוא רוחניותיהם . . . והשיג האדם בשכלו ידיעת הכליות ובהרגשות ידיעת האישים . . . דע כי המדע המוכרחי אשר הוא מוכרח האדם להודות אותו, ולא יוכל לכפר אותו שום משכיל בשום פנים, ואם יכפרני שום כופר, נחשוב אותו שאינו עומד על שלמות דעתו ויושר טבעו . . . . אין לך דבר גלוי יותר מאלה. ועל כן הביא הצורך להודות בהם ועל כן נקראו מדע מוכרחי . . . . המדע המופתי, והוא מדע הראיה, — הוא בנוי על המדע המוכרחי.

[12] Text p. 7 (beginning of ch. 2): דע, יאמצך הבורא, כי אמתת החומר ועניננו הוא שהוא יסוד לשום דבר ושום התחלה לדבר, ולולי זה לא היה החומר. וראיה לזה, כי כשתתבונן כל הדברים המעשיים והטבעיים מצאנו אותם לא ימלטו מחומר וצורה . . . אבל הדברים הרוחניים החומר להם כמו המין העליון, והצורה כמו המין השפל.

[13] Text pp. 7–19; note, p. 17. ולא יתכן לאדם הכח הזה האלוהי אלא להעמיד נפשו על אמתת הדברים ולעשות כל מה שיצוה השכל, כי השכל הוא העד הנאמן אשר העיד

like plants and animals, but he alone can master all arts and make all kinds of food: man's body is different from other creatures in that he is erect, for he is a unique plant in that he originates in heaven, and, his head, which is the root, faces heavenward.[14]

Since there is nothing in the outer-world that does not find its counterpart in the inner-world of man, ibn Zaddik states that man has a plant-soul and an animal-soul, but, because he is man, he possesses a rational soul which originates in heaven, the counterpart of his rational soul. The plant-soul and its powers are all a unit and all of them are spiritual powers derived from the universal powers in the upper world.[14] The animal-soul appears when the form of being is complete, and is carried in the spirit of the animal or man which is found in the pure blood of the arteries which have two membranes, with two passages, one for blood and one for the spirit or mind — but the seat of the animal-soul and its bearer is the pure red blood: — as evidence of this we see two receptacles in the heart — one for the spirit and one for the blood. The functions of this animal-soul are two-fold, namely, sensation and motion — and the latter may be active or passive: the active motions are those of the arteries and respiration, and the passive motions give rise to emotions of anger, fear, shame, joy, sorrow. After explaining the various emotions ibn Zaddik concludes by saying that without pain there is no pleasure and that pleasure varies in accordance with the antecedent pain.[15]

הבורא ית' על ברואיו. והואיל שהגענו עד המקום הזה נבאר הסבה אשר בשבילה יכלה ויסוף העולם הזה. ואל תעלה בדעתך כי באמרי שהעולם הזה אין לו עמידה ולא קיום — שרוצני העולם בכללו. אבל רצוני הדברים הנכללים תחת ההויה וההפסד שכבר זכרתי בתחלת השער השלישי: שהגלגל אינו נפסד ואינו משתנה ממה שהוטבע מרצון הבורא יתעלה. שכבר אמר הפילוסוף, שכל מה שנתנה לו השלמות בבת אחת לא יפסד, הואיל וראשיתו ואחריתו אחד.

[14] Text pp. 19–25, note especially, pp. 24 and 25, אבל האדם מפני שטבעו מיושר משאר נבראים . . . נזקפה קומתו . . . והעלה האחרת שהאדם צמח מן השמים, כלומר שכל צמח יצמח מעיקרו, ולפי שראש האדם הוא עיקרו ונהיה העיקר ממול השמים — לפיכך אנחנו צמח מן השמים . . . . האדם יותר מיושר בטבעו משאר בעלי חיים . . . והנה התבאר שיש לנפש הגידול וכחות: כח המציר, וכח הגידול וכח זן, והכח המציר ישלים פעולתה.

[15] Text pp. 28–31: הנפש החיה היא בלב, נשואה בדם הנקי המתולעי אשר בלב. והוא מה שאנו רואים בלב שני כיסים: באחד הרוח, בשני הדם . . . המוח הוא שורש העצבים, ובהתחלתם ובעצבים ישלמו הפעולות הבאות מן הבחירה . . . וענין השמחה שתצא הנפש לקראת הדבר ההוא ותמס ותנפץ והיה ממין העונג, אלא שהעונג יבא מעט מעט והשמחה בבת אחת כאשר בינון ובפחד.

A very significant statement of ibn Zaddik is that concerning life, which, he says, is the effect of the animal-soul: the disappearance of the effect does not mean that the cause disappears too, for death means only the separation of the soul, not the destruction of it. From this ibn Zaddik launches into a thorough discussion of the soul, which I shall treat separately.

Ibn Zaddik continues the discussion of soul with the exhortation that Man should reason and investigate. Much benefit is in store for him in the use of these, and the purpose of his existence becomes self-evident: these capacities distinguish him from animals. Man should deaden the animal desires. Quoting the prophets,[16] he stresses the idea that it is important to strive for the knowledge of God, for it is the highest knowledge and the cause of human perfection.[17] Ibn Zaddik goes into quite a refutation against the views of the Kalam and of Joseph al-Basir[18] and then gives his own views in the nature and existence of God. He approaches this discussion through an exposition of the four causes — material, formal, efficient and final. The reasoning and logic he builds up to establish his points of view lead him to no better conclusions than those of the Kalam.[19]

[16] Jer. 31.33: "They shall all know me, from the least of them even unto their greatest." Amos 5.6: "Seek for the Lord and you shall live." Hos. 6.3: "We may feel it, and strive to know the Lord." Isa. 30.11: "Get you out of the way, turn aside out of the path, cause the Holy One of Israel to cease from before us."

[17] Text pp. 33–43; note pp. 41 and 42 — חיוב העיון והדרישה לאדם דבר שיעידו עליו הראיות הנכתבות והמופתים השכליים . . .

[18] His book called "Mansuri" — See text pp. 43–47, esp. 44: טענה ראשונה מה שכתוב בספר הנקרא מנצ'ורי באמרו זה: הם שסברתם שאלהים ירד ויעלה שהם לא עבדו אלהים; ואני אומר, שהאומר דבר זה אומר אמת, אבל הם שכחו נפשם שהם אומרים שהלוה חפץ בחפץ מחודש, והאומר דבר זה לא עבד אלהים מעולם, ולא ידע אותו. Cf. also "Mahkimat Peti" of Joseph ha–Roeh.

[19] Text pp. 47–57: כל הדברים שיאהב האדם לעמוד עליהם ולהשיג אותם, יש לו לחקור עליהם מן הדרכים הארבעה שהם העילות הטבעיות: שהם העילה היסודית, והעילה הצוריית, והעילה הפועלת ועילת התכלית . . . . נמצא דרך החקירה לכל הנמצאים באלו עילות. ומי שבקש שום דבר באחת מהם השיג ידיעת הבורא ההוא. ומה שאין לו עילה, אלא שהוא עילת כל דבר, אין דרך ואין שביל לידיעתו . . . ומזה יתבאר לך שהבורא אינו ראוי לשאל עליו מהו, ולא איך הוא ולא איזה זמן הוא, שכל הדברים האלו דבקים בנמצאים שיש להם עילה, אבל הוא שאין לו עילה, אבל הוא עילת כל דבר, אין שואלין אלא אם הוא וזאת היא החקירה על אימות (פי' מלשון אם, כלומר: אם הוא) ועל אמתתו.

Although more systematic and more logical than Saadia and Bachya, ibn Zaddik proves the creation of the world, and, thereby the existence of a creator, from its finiteness. For ibn Zaddik the will of God has existed from all eternity, and, cannot be separated from the essence of God. Creation ignores time, and, therefore, before the production of the spheres time did not exist. This view as to the existence of God leads to the view of the uniqueness of God, who cannot be considered in his essence as a plurality — this would nullify his existence. God is to the created things as a unit is to other numbers, — forming and comprising them, yet, in essence, quite different:[20] divine attributes follow from God's unity,[21] and he concludes that no positive attributes, whether essential or unessential, can be posited of God, who is undefinable — and — it is more proper to apply negative attributes to God than positive.[22]

Ibn Zaddik concludes his treatise with the fourth division and treats of the duties of man, reward and punishment, and resurrection. He emphasizes the fact of the goodness inherent in the Commandments of God — they are, like the act of our creation, for our own good, even though we may not realize it: man should serve God with all his heart and carry out all His precepts. Man needs these Commandments — they were made especially for him, for how can God reward a person in the world to come for that which he had not done: man has the freedom to choose and determine their conduct — hence, reward and punishment are just. It behooves man, therefore, to imitate God and be good, merciful and kind. A knowledge of God is essential for it leads to conscious practice of the good and results in a reward for man in the world to come. With Plato, ibn Zaddik reminds man that he should regard three things — firstly, that there is a Creator who protects all and disposes of everything; secondly, that nothing can be hidden from God; and, lastly, that man

[20] Contra Saadia and Bachya and like Maimonides.

[21] P. 51: היחוד האמתי שהוא עצמו ועצמו ית', שאחד המספר אינו כאחד האלהות, שהאחד המספר יש בו רבוי ויחייבוהו החילוק והכפל, אבל יחוד האלהות הוא נפרד מעצמו.

[22] Text pp. 57–58: אבל היחוד הזה אשר לאלה האמתי לא ישכיל האדם ממנו יותר ממה שתראה... בהיות עצמו יקר מכל העצמים, כן מדותיו יקרות מכל המדות. ואין מדותיו חוץ מעצמו, ולא עצמו זולת מדותיו, אבל זה במדות יחוד אמתי, לא יכנס בו שום טעות...

cannot win the favor of God through sacrifices, but, must win God over to himself by good deeds. These good deeds and goodness and virtue are based on the knowledge of God's attributes, on righteousness and justice, hope and humility.[23] The evil in the world, to the righteous, is a natural occurrence and is in no way connected with reward and punishment; however, there are incidents where a particular evil is inflicted upon the good man so as to forgive his sins. Reward and punishment is for the future life, is spiritual, and reward and punishment is, therefore, timeless. Ibn Zaddik finally concludes his treatise with a discussion of the Messianic time, when the pious man and those who died for the sanctification of God's name will be brought back to life and will never die again — living like Moses on the divine mountain and basking in the divine light.[24]

2. *The Soul.*

Ibn Zaddik emphasized the psychical man more than he did the physical man. He uses the tripartite division of soul, — man, he says, is made up of three souls — the vegetative, animal

[23] See text pp. 62–65: והתבאר בביאור זה פנים אחרים שיצר את האדם כדי לעשות מצוותיו, ועשות מצוותיו כדי ליתן להם שכר, שהוא הטוב, וזה היה חפץ הבורא בבראו את האדם, וזה הוא מה שבקש ממנו . . . וא"ת: היתכן שיזכו לשכר טוב מבלי מצוות, אשיבך: לא יהיה אז מדין החכמה ליתן שכר טוב מי שלא יזכה . . . וא"ת: שהרשע הזה היה בדעת הבורא שעתיד להכעיסו ויתחייב להענישו לעולם, למה ברא אותו . . . נשיבך, שלא יחייב להכעיס הבורא ית' מפני שהיה יודע הבורא שיכעיסוהו . . . שהאדם השלם החסיד כשיכיר את בוראו וידע לו שהוא קדום לו יותר מנפשו . . . וישער עצמות אלקיו ית' . . . ויותר מכל נעימות הבורא ית' וחסדו שעשה עמו, שהזהירו וציוהו על עבודתו והעידהו לעשות רצונו: מי המגיע למעלה הזאת הוא המשובח לאדוניו ומשתעבד לו תמיד בסתר ובגלוי, והסתלקו ממנו התאוות הגשמיות והבחירות הרעות והוא בכל זה הענין אוהב את בוראו שהשפיע עליו כל הטובות האלה . . . וכן אמר הפלוסוף אפלטון שלשה דברים . . . האחד מהם, שיש לדברים ממציא והוא אחד . . . והשני, שהבורא לא יסתר ממנו דבר . . . והשלישי, שלא יתרצה לאדם בהקריבו קרבנות, אבל יתרצה בעשותו מעשים טובים. He quotes many other Biblical sources, as Jer. 9.23: "I am the Lord who exercises kindness, justice, and righteousness on the earth; for in these things I delight, saith the Lord." Also, Zeph. 2.3: "Seek ye the Lord, all ye meek of the earth, who have fulfilled His ordinances; seek righteousness, seek meekness." Compare these four qualities with the four cardinal virtues expressed by Plato.

[24] Text pp. 59–79; note pp. 78–79: . . . והצדיקים חיים לראות ולהורות את בוראם יושבים ומתעננים מזיו השכינה . . . אור זרוע לצדיק ולישרי לב שמחה.

and rational, and, of these, the rational is the highest in quality and is spiritual in substance and its accidents, — as for example, justice, benevolence, conception, etc. On the other hand, injustice, malice, and imbecility, etc., are not accidents, but, rather, are negations of justice, benevolence, and conception.[25] In the line of this method man, from the knowledge of his physical self, derives his understanding of the material world, as does he derive his conception of the spiritual world only through his soul. A happy blending of both methods, the physical and psychical, leads to a full understanding of God — the Creator.

The above may be said to be the premise, if you please, of the whole discussion of the *Soul* of ibn Zaddik. Of course, he employs the definition of soul as given by Aristotle,[26] and he elaborates in defining still more the definition of Aristotle. For example, in line with the discussion at the beginning of this part of the chapter, he says "substance" excludes the thought that the soul is an accident: by "giving perfection" is meant, that, through which man himself, through his soul, becomes perfect, and, through which man is able to enter the next world. In this way, man fulfills the purpose not only of his creation and composition of his body, but the creation of matter too. Likewise, ibn Zaddik takes the phrase "natural organic body" and says that it implies that the body is an organon, an instrument

[25] Truly a Neo-Platonic doctrine; note page 38: והנפש החכמה עצם והיא נושאה המקרים בהכרח, אבל המקרים של הנפש החכמה הכל רוחניים כמו שהעצם הזה רוחניי, ומקרה הנפש הזאת: המדע והחסד והטוב והיושר ושאר המדות הדומות לאלו. ואם יאמר שום אדם: ואיך הנחת הסכלות והעולה והרע ושאר ההפכים, כלומר — הפך אלו הנזכרים? נאמר לו: המדות האלה הנזכרים נבראו עמו, אבל המדות האלו האחרונות אינם הפכים לאלה אבל הם אפיסה, כאפיסת הראות, אפיסת העין ואפיסת העושר, שאינו הפך העושר אבל אפיסתו.

[26] Pp. 36–37: וראה איך אמר הפילוסוף במליצת משלו, בשומו רשם הנפש שהיא עצם מתמים לגוף טבעי כלי בעל חיות בכח. וענין „הרשם הזה" הוא מעילה ורחוק מעילה ומה שאמר על הנפש שהיא „עצם" להבדילה ממקרה, ומה שאמר מתמים: ר"ל שהעצם הזה היא עילה מתמימת לאדם, הואיל והיא סיבה לעולם הבא, הואיל ובגלל הטוב הזה נבראנו. ואמר: גשם טבעי כלי, שהוא כלי שתשתמש בו הנפש לפי חפצה וכוונתה הואיל ואין לגוף שום חפץ, ומפני היותו חסר הופקד עליו להנהיגו עצם שלם . . . As quoted in other chapters of this volume, this definition is from Aristotle's de Anima II: I 412 b4. Compare Saadia, Halevi, and ibn Daud.

in the due process of soul — functioning where the soul uses the body to carry out its own purposes. He says in a summary way that the rational soul is like a king and the animal soul is like an official before the king, admonishing the appetitive soul.[27] However, we should understand, says ibn Zaddik, that these *souls* are spiritual powers with inherent benefit to the body, with the rational soul at command, which rational soul, when perfected, that is, developed from potential intellect, becomes intellect: degree and excellence differentiate the rational soul from intellect. From this point ibn Zaddik employs, somewhat, the Neo-Platonic doctrine of emanation when he refers to the "World of Intellect" as being superior, with its matter as being the "pure light," an "intellect" wherein there is no ignorance for it comes from God without intermediate agency.[28] Therefore, the primary function of the rational soul is to raise itself from its potential and attain knowledge — to investigate the unknown and to comprehend it: man alone can utilize this soul, and attain general rules, make premises and infer one thing from another.[29] There is a universal soul which embraces all the individual souls, thereby specifying each individual soul with the soul-character which is common to all individual souls.

[27] To be sure, as stated in the beginning of this chapter, ibn Zaddik illustrates here the free use of a distinctly scientific definition of *Soul* which Aristotle uses in his "De Anima." One can readily see the combination of Platonic and Neo-Platonic psychology applied to the Aristotelian definition of soul. Note p. 37: והנפש החכמה כמו המלך, והנפש החיה כמו שוטר ונוגש המשרת את פני המלך והיא הנוערת בנפש התאוה ובכחות המתאוים. See note in Schmiedl, *loc. cit.*, pp. 145–146.

[28] P. 37: ומפני שהנפש החכמה מין לנפשות האלו הנשארות, נקראו נפשות, כמו שיקרא הדבר על שם מינו. ואם יאמר שום אדם: ומפני־מה נקרא השכל נפש והוא עצם עומד לעצמו ויקום לנפש לשום תועלת? נאמר לו, שהנפש החכמה שכל בכח ואין ביניהם חלוף אלא במעלה ויתרון, ושעולם השכל יותר מעולה — לא עלוי מקומי, אבל עילוי שררה ויתרון, שהחמר שלו האור התם והזוהר הבהיר, השכל אשר אין לו סכלות, לפי שהוא יוצא מגבורת הבורא ית' בלי אמצעות.

[29] P. 38: ... ידע באמת שהנפש הזאת מכרת וחוקרת והיא תשיג הדברים שהם מושכלים, ותוציא הכללים ותקדים ההקדמות ותלמוד דבר מדבר. ואין אנו רואים מעלה זו לאחד מבעלי החיים אלא לאדם לבדו... השכל הוא בנפש בכח, ויוציאהו האדם ברוב הרגל ולמוד מן הכוח אל הפועל, ואלו לא היה השכל בנפש לא בכוח ולא בפועל — הוא הנמנע.

The essence of the universal soul is one and indivisible despite the fact that it may be divided into many individual souls.[30] In this, ibn Zaddik emphasizes the fact, that man is capable of choosing the true as against the false light: man, if pure and wise, can receive the virtues of justice and righteousness as against evil and wrong: praise and reward or blame, and, punishment, may be his portion to the extent of which he applies himself to the task and privilege of appropriating the essence of the universal soul. Man is destined, therefore, through his rational soul, for the spiritual world, which is pure and perfect, and not subject to change, defect, or need, and it is simple and spiritual. This world that God created, is not created for His need, but, rather, to show His goodness and power: it behooves man to reason and investigate, in order to gain the benefits from this goodness and power of God and, also, thus fulfill the purpose of his existence.[31]

3. *Reflective Analysis.*

Upon careful perusal and a like introspection of the thoughts expressed by Joseph ibn Zaddik in his "Olam Katon," one finds the soul of a true mystic who desires to put into daily practice the yearnings of his heart and mind towards communion with the infinite. To ibn Zaddik this manifestation of divine communion is very real and this is the first point I desire to stress here. Ibn Zaddik sees no future for the man who does not develop his rational soul from the potential stage to the universal intellect. It is important for human beings to be cognizant of their inherent power — a power arising from the rational soul,

[30] P. 40: כל מה שידין השכל על נפש אחת עבר דינו על הנפש הכולות (פי' הכוללת) בכללה, שהויה ההיא מדרך היותה עצם רוחני, לא גוף ולא ממלא גוף ולא נכלל תחת הזמן. והואיל והתבאר זה נבאר שיש שם עולם רוחני כנגד העולם הזה הגשמי ושהוא יותר שלם ממנו.

[31] Pp. 40–41: שהנפש הזאת החכמה היא ערוכה לאותו העולם ר"ל שתכליתה לעולם הרוחני אחר הפרדה מן הגוף כמו שהגוף הזה ערוך לעולם הזה הגשמי, וכמו שהעולם הזה חסר אפס מטובה כן העולם ההוא עולם מלא מטובות ומשפיע טובות, לפי שהבורא ית' מאציל עליו האור האמתי בלי כלי אמצעות ונתן לו השלמות בבת אחת, והוא מאציל עליו האור האמתי בלי אמצעות לפיכך לא ישיגהו שנוי ולא חסרון...

to ever increasingly grow in strength so as to appropriate more and more of the "Universal Intellect." Just how important this is ibn Zaddik stresses the fact that in the absence of such growth and development of the rational soul, man, would be nothing more than a beast, perhaps less, since the beast never falls below his animal nature; therefore, ibn Zaddik exhorts man to exert his prerogative and privilege in order that he may live and not die.[32]

Closely allied to the above exhortation that man develop his rational soul is the insistence that knowledge just for its own sake is not sufficient. A very practical end in attaining knowledge is given to us by ibn Zaddik. We should deaden our animal desires and lead our rational soul to a knowledge, not to much of the corporeal world, but, rather, to a full knowledge of the existence of a spiritual world. This is the true knowledge, and, man is thus enabled to know the Creator, who is the only real existent. In all ages there is a need of reminding men to recall to themselves the aim and purpose of their real existence; this, one can do through reflection and contemplation upon the One real existent: ibn Zaddik surely must have been fraught with great perplexities as we are today. His insistence that we reach within ourselves surely is the note of the mystic, and this note one senses throughout his treatise. Therefore, the end of all knowledge, the highest knowledge, is the knowledge of God: to attain this knowledge gives man the power to enjoy artistic contemplation and cause him to be ever-increasingly perfect.[33]

[32] Pp. 40–43: חיוב העיון והדרישה לאדם דבר שיעידו עליו הראיות הנכתבות והמופתים השכליים . . . שלא נברא האדם רק להתלמד . . .

[33] Text pp. 23–43; note pp. 23 and 24: לפי שהנפש צריכה לגוף להשלים פעולתה, ולא ישלים לגוף גידול אלא בנפש הצומחת, שהגוף הוא דבר מת כמו האבן וזולתה, וידוע שהאדם אינו כן. Note also above, notes to text of pp. 59–69; cf. also text, pp. 66–67: והנה שיש לנו העיקר הגדול מן העבודה בחכמה, שבגללה נברא האדם ועל־כן הותרו בו המקרים, הראשונים והעצמים הראשונים — להורות ולהתלמד בהם על העצמים השניים . . . והראיה שהאדם נברא בגלל החכמה: שהאדם לא נברא אלא להשיג טעם העולם הבא . . . אם־כן הבראתו ועילת המצאו לא היו כי אם בחכמה, ובגלל החכמה ידעו הדברים הכוליים הנצחיים . . . וראוי למצטדק לדעת מדותיו ושמותיו ישתבח, — לא שידע אישי השמות המוגשמות המורגשות בלבד, מבלי שידע הענינים הרוחניים.

Even though ibn Zaddik was Neo-Platonic in his view regarding the soul and its accidents, still we have a most important contribution from him in that he stresses the fact that the accidents of the soul are spiritual, as is the soul itself.[34] This is a most practical point, and my humble experience points to the need today in making this point clear, as well as stressing it to the inquisitive public and to the questioning parishioners. As was stated in the beginning of the discussion of the soul in this chapter, this point may be called the premise of the whole discussion of soul-development of ibn Zaddik. When we speak of conception, justice, kindness, and goodness, and other qualities of like nature, we may call them eternal verities — spiritual values. However, imbecility, wrong, malice, and evil are not the opposites of those mentioned above and were not simultaneously created with the soul like the positive accidents: they are merely the "absence" of the positive qualities — God did not create nor desire any evil or defects. This point is so strong in our own Jewish theology that it has become an essential part of our liturgy:[35] a challenge to the theory of original sin and an exhortation to the effect that God did not create any evil, any defect, nor any negative phase of life. What an opportunity there is within each one of us to strive to reinstate ourselves to our original self when we find ourselves attached to things and events, corporeal and material! Is it not within our province to ask man to turn his mind from evil so that he may see the good?

[34] Note the following: p. 31: כמו שהתקשרה החיה בגוף אחר שהתקשר הצמחונית ואחר שישלים דינה, כן תדבק החכמה בחיה אחר התקשר החיה בצמחונית ואחר שתשלים פעולתה. P. 33: ונספר עכשיו שהנפש החכמה דבר אחד זולתי הגוף ואינה ג״כ מטבע הגוף ואינה בתוך הגוף ולא חוצה לו, אבל היא יותר דבקה בו דבוק דיוקי ויורנו זה שהנפש אינה גוף. p. 34: והואיל והתבאר שהנפש אינה ממין הגוף, נבאר אחר־זה שהנפש אינה מקרה. p. 38, as noted above: אבל המקרים של הנפש החכמה הם רוחניים, כמו שהעצם הוא רוחני.

[35] Note for example the prayer, "My God, the soul which Thou hast given unto me came pure from Thee. Thou hast created it, Thou hast formed it, Thou hast breathed it into me; Thou hast preserved it in this body and, at the appointed time, Thou wilt take it from this earth that it may enter upon life everlasting. While the soul animates my being, I will worship Thee, Sovereign of the world, and Lord of all souls. Praised be Thou, O Lord, in whose hands are the souls of all living and the spirits of all flesh."

Ibn Zaddik quotes the prophets who search for God, but these prophets, likewise, exhort us to cleanse ourselves and return from evil and live.[36]

We may, with a fair degree of certainty, say that ibn Zaddik broached the realm of individual responsibility regarding the field of soul-development. Surely the rational soul is the only field of the microcosm of man in which is found the germ of self-development, self-discipline, and self-realization. The use of this rational soul on the part of man is obligatory and the abuse thereof a shame and a reproach. In the insistence of this point ibn Zaddik does surely give us a tool for not only character and soul development, but, also, an intimation of the immortality of the soul. The spiritual world, fine and perfect as it is, was made by God without an intermediate agency: man can become part of this spiritual world through his own agency; no one can nor may intercede for him: it depends upon man himself to so properly have his rational soul function that its destination for the spiritual world is assured and certain.[37] We should bear in mind, too, that ibn Zaddik intimates to us that, in this struggle and development of the rational soul, from potentiality to actuality, that man has accepted frailties of our common nature: this, however, is not to be misconstrued as implying original sin, rather, to the condition and influence of the animal soul. It is the proximity and predominance of the corporeal world that causes man to err: the rational soul gives existence to the animal soul, and man's life itself is ultimately derived from this rational soul. It is incumbent upon man, through study, to make the rational soul actual — this gives man his

[36] Note above p. 47, n. 16 in re Jeremiah, Amos, and Hosea. See also Ezek. 33.11: "Say unto them, as I live, saith the Lord God, I have no pleasure in the death of the wicked, but that the wicked turn from his way and live: turn, ye, turn ye from your evil ways; for why will ye die, O house of Israel."

[37] Pp. 40–41: ועילת העולם הרוחני הוא האל האמת שחדשהו בכחו . . . אבל הבורא אין תכליתו לאחריתו לפי שאי אפשר להיות יותר שלם ממה שהוא ויותר תם, שהוא רוחני פשוט . . . וכן תדע שהטוב כלו יגיע אלינו משם והאור ולולי האור המגיע אלינו מן הגלגלים היה העולם חשך אפילה, בלי שום אור, שהחשך אינו כ"א על הארץ, וכן כל הטובות והחסדים זרים הם בעולם הזה. ישתבח הבורא אשר בראנו להשתבח בתהלתי.

reason through which man exerts his purposiveness in learning to choose between good and evil, to go the right way and win salvation — and, live. In the life that man "wins" for himself he finds many paths through which he reaches the highways of meditation, the blissfulness and the blessedness of artistic contemplation and — the superior gift of communion with the divine.[38]

[38] Moses ibn Tibbon, the Translator of "Olam Katan" fittingly closes his work with the following poem:

לאלי אתן שיר ידידים
עזרני להשלים דברי חמודים
ישלח לעמו השדודים
מלאכיו עולים ויורדים
זה לזה מצמידים
לחזק ידי מ ש ה הכבדים.

VIII.

JUDAH HALEVI — 1095–1145.

1. *Life and Works.*[1]

Judah Halevi's is a record of an incarnation of a poetic spirit who spoke the word of God and lived it in as thorough a fashion. He was born in Toledo the latter part of the eleventh century. He studied at the Jewish center of Lucena, acquainting himself with the Talmud and other important sources. Alfasi had a great influence upon him and cultivated the healthful and edifying friendships of Joseph Migash and Baruch Albalia. His poetic genius made itself felt early in life — his livelihood, however, he made through the practice of medicine. He later went to Cordova and became very prominent and well-liked as a physician. He found much time to write poetry and the contents of these were chiefly concerned with his intense love for his persecuted people and ardent enthusiasm for the proposition that the land of Palestine should again become the home of his people. His cherished hope was to visit and live in Palestine — this made him travel to various cities enroute thereto — and legend has it that after many cordial receptions in different cities he did reach the holy city and while he was offering up the song of Zion, his own ode, he was killed by an Arab horseman.[2]

Halevi had a poetic soul — although he emphasized reason as a necessary and very important part of man's endowment, still, when it comes to Judaism and the discussion of the nature of God, reason alone cannot answer many of the perplexing

[1] See Kaufmann, *loc. cit.* for Halevi's life and works where a more complete and comprehensive account may be obtained.

[2] Many versions are extant. The late Prof. Jacob Mann believed that Halevi returned home and lived there till his natural death.

questions.[3] The laws of logic, mathematics and science are good in themselves but, there is a certain transcendental knowledge and gift needed in order to understand God — this gift is given to a few — the Jewish people who, through the study and appreciation of their Torah and tradition obtain a love of God and can have God reveal Himself to them in the land of Palestine.[4] Israel among the nations is just like the heart in the body. Israel has a different mixture, disposition and combination. It takes "Jewish blood" to produce a prophet — which, to Halevi, is the highest attainment of the soul. Truly, this is the purpose of his whole book entitled "Al Khazari"[5] — an apologetic treatise in defence of the Jewish religion and tradition and to justify that the Jews are a chosen people.[6] To expatiate upon the above he wrote his book in the form of a dialogue between the King of the Khazars and a Jewish Rabbi in which the King is converted to Judaism. Emphasis upon Jewish tradition, defence of the Talmud, explanation of the developmental and vitalizing effect of the "Divine Influence," a thorough discussion of divine names and attributes are given, rites and ceremonies upheld and a thorough examination of the nature of the human soul. The treatment is strong and convincing. The book had the desired effect. It influenced many writers that followed[7] and went through several editions in the Hebrew.[8] True it is that Halevi's fame as a philosopher was overshadowed by the fact that he was a great poet and the latter appealed to a larger public but his "Kuzari" remained, for a very long time, the source of inspiration and information for many generations to come.

[3] As to the influence upon Halevi by Al Gazali, see Kaufmann's *Geschichte der Attributenlehre in der Religionsphilosophie des Mittelalters*, Gotha, 1877, pp. 119–140.

[4] Kuzari (ed. Vilna, 1914) II, pp. 12–16, IV, p. 11.

[5] The text used in this treatise is that of the Hebrew translation by Judah ibn Tibbon, ed., Vilna, 1914.

[6] What has been said of Saadia in re: combating the Karaites and other sects may be said of Halevi who defends tradition and the Talmud.

[7] Abraham b. Ezra, Abraham b. Daud and many others.

[8] Maimuni's "Guide" appeared thirty years later but did not overshadow the "Kuzari."

2. *The Soul.*

It is in the Fifth Part of the Kuzari that we find Halevi's discussion and elaboration of the concept of the soul. It embraces an extensive criticism of the "Kalam" as well as of the Karaites. The King admits his dissatisfaction and restlessness of soul as a result of the conversations with the philosopher, the Christian and the Mohammedan. The Rabbi agrees to satisfy the King but with different methods than those given by the Karaites and others. The Rabbi refuses to delve into metaphysics without intermediate steps. — He plans, rather, to dissect for the King the general organization of the physical and transcendental worlds and thus explain the nature of the Soul, etc.[9] Halevi, in this Part attempts to prove that the rational soul can exist without a body.[10] We have travelled far in our discussion of the Soul. The conception of the soul as a substance derived from the luminous primal matter, like the heavenly spheres and the angels, was held by all the philosophers up to now and based their proofs of immortality thereon. The Platonic doctrine of pre-existence was gradually discarded because of the Aristotelian theory that the Soul is the form-principle of the body was more acceptable; the theory that the Soul's existence may be ascribed to a creative act of God at the birth of the child or at its conception was the one destined to become the more plausible. However, Halevi, staunch and pious, vigorously emphasized the indivisibility of the soul, its incorporeality, its reality apart from the condition of the body and — contrary to the Aristotelian adherents — who believed that soul would be absorbed in the divine soul, the active intellect — Halevi emphasized the immortality of the individual as a fundamental article of faith.[11] To Halevi, Divine Influence is form-giving

[9] Part V, P. 2: ... לא אנהג בך על דרך הקראים, אשר עלו אל החכמה האלהית מבלי מדרגה, אבל אקרב לך ראשי דברים יעזרוך בציור ההיולי והצורה, ואחר כן היסודות ... ואחר כן הנפש, ואחר כן השכל, ואחר כן החכמה האלהית.

[10] *Ibid.*: ואתן לך ראיות מספיקות שאין הנפש המדברת צריכה לגוף.

[11] Part V, p. 12. — This whole paragraph could well be quoted as a whole, for it gives one of the best summaries of a soul concept. Suffice here to give his premise and I refer the reader to a careful study of the rest: יתבאר מציאותו הנפש בתנועות וההרגש לחיים שונה מן התנועות היסודיות, ונקרא סבתם נפש או כח נפשי.

Intelligence of all things and elements, and it is this Influence that arranges, motivates and clarifies the concepts of matter and form, quantity and quality and the other accidents or combination of accidents. It is the Divine Influence that creates the variations in degree and kind in animal, plant and human life. Halevi gives a beautiful illustration of the seed[12] and its limitations which, pursues a course known as nature — so called by philosophers. This nature[13] has powers which guard the preservation of the species, since the *essence* of the individual cannot be preserved, it being composed of various component parts.[14] Such thing is devoid of the power of motion and is guided by Nature. God is the one who controls it in a certain extent and condition whether you call the latter nature, soul, power or angel. The mixtures may vary in the degrees of refinement and the Divine Wisdom may favour any one mixture with a higher form above the mere physical power — this *form* allotted to it above its physical life is called *Soul*.[15] Now every soul uses its faculties according to its nature but nature does not reach perfection in any *part* of animal life and thus there is no desire for greater form than that of the living *Soul*.[16] With man, however, it is possible to reach higher development — the Divine Influence gives him the power to develop from the material or passive intellect within him to a higher and more perfect soul. Man yearns for a distinct and divine character above his own — this makes him walk in and choose the right path — upon him is the prophetic spirit poured out and he is able to appropriate it. However, if he is not fully master of himself he can only reach the stage of inspiration — and not, as in the former case, the stage of prophecy. Man has within himself the faculty known as the Active Intellect — this is his unique characteristic and

[12] See V, P. 10, p. 29, cf. I, p. 72: הנקראת אצלם טבע. והוא כח משתדל בשמירת המין: בעבור שלא היה אפשר להשאר האיש ההוא בעצמו. שהוא מורכב מדברים משתנים.

[13] Part V, P. 10 — a most important paragraph of profound philosophical content and anticipating much of modern philosophical discussion.

[14] Part V, P. 10, p. 29.

[15] *Ibid.*, p. 30: ונקראת הצורה הנתונה לו יתירה על הטבע נפש.

[16] *Ibid.*, p. 31: וכל נפש תכסוף להשתמש בכחותיה כאשר הוכנו לה, ולא נשתנו הטבעיים במאומה מן החי הבהמי. ואיננו בכסף לקבול צורה יתירה על הנפש החיונית. אבל נשתנו באדם ונכספו לצורה יתירה.

he can, thereby, attain the supreme and superb stage of being an angel below God and he may truly be said to be in Paradise and as having acquired lasting life.[17]

The above, is, in short, a brief summary of Halevi's idea of the Soul development. Later[18] he goes into a very interesting and instructive discussion of the existence and nature of soul with its inherent faculties and powers[19] as he calls them. To Halevi, the existence of the soul is shown in living beings by motion and perception in contradistinction to the movements of the elements. The "*Soul*," or "animal power" is the *cause* of the motion and perception of the living beings. This cause is divided into three distinct phases, namely, vegetative power which is common to animal and plant life; vital power which is common to man and the other living beings, and, lastly, rational power, specifically characteristic of man.[19] The actions as issuing from the forms of matter give us an idea of the nature of the soul — the *form* of the living being is its *soul*; the knife, as Halevi says, does not cut because it is substance, but because it has the *form* of a knife; its cutting is its *soul*, and living is the soul of man.[20] These individualities, these various forms, are, perfections (entelechies) — they give the structures perfection, — and the *soul*, which is the functioning element, may truly be called a perfection.[21] There are two distinct perfections; one is primary, which gives the principle of actions, and the other, the secondary, is the nature of the actions which arise out of the principle. The importance of the above is in the conclusion that Halevi comes to in saying that the *Soul* is a primary perfection,[21] because it is a principle from which some-

[17] *Ibid.*, p. 33: והפילוסופים קוראים נותן המדרגה הזאת: השכל הפועל, וישימוהו מלאך אחרי האלהים. וכאשר שכלי בני אדם נדבקים בו הוא גן עדנם והתמדתם הנצחית.

[18] *Ibid.*, P. 12 — a most instructive discussion and well worth the time for the student to ponder over.

[19] *Ibid.*, p. 34, vegetative power הכח הצמחי, vital power, הכח החיוני, and rational power, הכח הזכרי

[20] Truly Aristotelian. See *ibid.*, p. 34: כי הסכין לא יחתוך מצד שהוא גוף אבל מצד שיש לו צורת הסכין. וכן החי לא ירגיש וינוע מצד שהוא גוף. אך שיש לו צורת החיות, והיא הנקראת נפש.

[21] *Ibid.* p. 34–35: ונקראו אלו הצורות שלימות כי בהם ישלטו תכונות הדברים. והנפש שלמות . . . הנפש שלמות ראשון.

thing else (i. e. a second entelechy) may spring forth. It is this entelechy that is the determining factor either to a corporate object or to amorphous matter. The *Soul* is entelechy to a corporate object[22] and the latter may either be natural or artificial. The peculiarity of the *soul* is in the fact that it is a first entelechy to a natural corporate object.[23]— From the latter Halevi comes to his splendid summary statement of the concept of soul after he distinguished between organic and inorganic natural corporate object and says: The Soul is entelechy to a natural corporate object, endowed with organs and potentially with life, that is, a main-spring of potentially vivified actions, or susceptible to such.[24]

On the basis of the above Halevi gives a masterly discussion on the reality and indivisibility of the soul.[25] He leads up to this from the analysis of the theoretical and practical reasons; the former is activity of the rational soul in the fields of science and the latter its activity in subduing animal instinct.[26] Both cooperate, in the true man, to establish an intimate connection with the universal reason giving to such human being inspiration and revelation. This content of reason — is what gives form to the soul — and the *form* of the corporeal object — the soul in this condition is incorporeal and not an accident and therefore, by virtue of these, the soul cannot be divided like a corporeal object. Its primary tools are those spiritual forms which shape themselves in the center of the brain from the psychical spirit by means of the power of the imagination. A proof, furthermore, that the soul is distinct from the body, and does not require it, is to be found in the circumstance that the physical powers are weakened by strong influences — not so with the

[22] *Ibid.*, p. 35: והנפש שלמות לגשם.

[23] *Ibid.*, p. 35: והנפש שלמות לגשם טבעי.

[24] *Ibid.*, p. 35: והנפש שלמות ראשון לגשם טבעי כליי בעל חיות בכח, ר"ל מוצא הפעולות החיוניות בכח ומכין אותם.

[25] *Ibid.*, pp. 55–56: וממופתי עצמיות הנפש שהיא איננה גשם ולא מקרה, וכשהיא צורת הגשם לא תתחלק עצמותה בהתחלק הגשם.

[26] *Ibid.*, p. 55: והנפש המדברת כשהיא מקבילה אל החכמות נקראת פעולתה שכל עיוני. וכאשר היא מקבילה לגבור הכחות הבהמיים נקראת פעולתה הנהגה. ונקראת שכל מעשי.

soul.[27] The soul does not gain its knowledge empirically[28] as certain faculties of sight and motion are given to the body.

3. *Reflective Analysis.*

From the foregoing we find that Halevi did contribute much to our general subject of soul development. It is a wholesome presentation and conducive towards creating within man a desire for progress, attainment and perfection.

For convenience sake, I may say, that Halevi puts a challenge to man in the first part of his treatise, and this challenge starts the whole discussion of the beliefs and opinions of the various religions. The challenge is one of creed versus ritual or the intention of the heart versus ritual practices — as is said in the opening paragraph[29] — "Thy way of thinking is pleasing to God, but thy way of acting is not." Reflection and study made him (the King of the Khazars) accept Judaism — and — the *soul*, mind, divine influence and prophecy form a very important part of the discussion that follows the above challenge.

After analyzing the treatise of Halevi and reflecting thereon, I have come to the conclusion that he presents a distinct element of soul development. He does emphasize the existence of the two world orders — the natural and the spiritual and holds out the possibility of man's soul to develop into a high state of perfection and divinity[30] — this results from a "dual" relationship between man and God, and, God and Man. There is an essence and a process in this whole series of causation, in this whole relationship between God and Man. Within the limits we have the possibility of growth and development. — Man — who stands as the highest form of God's creation is endowed with a *soul* and this soul is his functioning element, his "form principle," if you please. This he can use or abuse and he takes

[27] *Ibid.*, p. 57–8: ומן הראיות על הפרד הנפש מהגוף ושאיננה צריכה אליו: כי הכחות הגשמיות יחלשו במושגיהם החזקים . . . והנפש המדברת אינה כך.

[28] *Ibid.*, p. 59: הוא שהנפש אין מדעיה הווים לה בנסיון.

[29] Part I, p. 1: כונתך רצויה ומעשיך אינם רצויים.

[30] See the discussion of the kinds of causation in Part V, P. 20. There are four kinds — natural, accidental, divine, and volitional.

the consequences accordingly. This is, in brief, the summary of Halevi's point of view. However, it is necessary in this reflective analysis to emphasize and re-state the salient points.

Firstly we should take up the inter-related subject of prophecy and nature. Halevi defines *nature*[31] at the outset and says the laws of nature comprise nurture, growth and propagation, with their powers and all conditions attached thereto[32] — but the soul, which is given to all living beings, functions differently in various living beings, and, particularly in man, who has a unique privilege and equipment to rise above and come into a separate and fifth class — namely — the Prophet (Note 31), Reason helps him to attain this stage, which varies in degree and kind. Man helps in this process — and the prophet, to Halevi, is a higher species of mortal — he is produced by the same principles of nature as given above but has an inner eye.[33] This man sees certain things that are invisible to the ordinary man; the immaterial objects are seen by him as are the material objects by the ordinary man — these spiritual and immaterial objects are real to the prophets, and an unbroken chain of tradition and prophets testify to this reality. This idea of reality and value is different than that of Bachya (and Maimuni and Saadia) whose test was pure rationality. To him the important laws are those known as rational commandments, — and, the purity of motive and intention — to Halevi, however, the premise is as stated above;[34] כונה is not alone necessary[35] but practice too; may I say, creativity resulting from the proper

[31] Part I, P. 73: In answer to [ומה הוא הטבע] Halevi's answers: כי הוא ההתחלה והסבה אשר בה ינוח וינוע הדבר אשר הוא בו בעצם ולא במקרה.

[32] Part I, Ps. 31–41: בדין הענין הטבעי נתחייב לקיחת המזון והגידול וההולדה וכחותם וכל תנאיהם . . . ובענין הנפש התיחדו בעלי חיים כלם, ונתחייבו מהם תנועות וחפצים ומדות וחושים נראים ונסתרים ותאוות, וזולת אלה . . . ובדין השכלי התיחד המדבר מכל החיים, והתחייב ממנו כל תקון המדות והמעון והמדינה ושאר הנהגות ונמוסים מנהגיים.

[33] Part IV, P. 3, pp. 32–33: ושם למי שבחר מברואיו עין נסתרת רואה דברים בעיניהם ולא יתחלפו. ויקח מהם [או: לסבותם] השכל ראיה על ענין הדברים ההם ולבותם ומי שנבראה לו העין ההיא הוא הפקח באמת . . . ואפשר שיהיו העינים ההם הכח המדמה בעוד שישמש הכח השכלי ותראינה צורות גדולות נוראות מורות על אמתות שאין בהם ספק . . . רצוני לומר כל הנביאים.

[34] Part II, Ps. 48–51.

[35] Part I, P. 17.

combinations of the various ingredients.[36] The prophet is the result of a thoroughgoing essence and process of development with the soul of man as the dynamic spark which helps man rise continually towards the degree of prophecy. Truly, this process, this relationship with God is not constant for some do and some do not become prophets.

Halevi imposes a wholesome life and creativity upon man in order that he reach a *full* development of his soul — in this he is truly human and he thus makes room for the play of all powers and faculties within man.[37] Man *develops* not through separation but through *activity*, and this activity is prompted by a desire on the part of man to make his soul reach the realm of prophecy — the realm of the higher being; those who live in the world of the spirit. Prayer alone does not accomplish this high degree; the soul must be fed with things spiritual, self-control, self-examination, the observance of festivals and commandments.

The last and nevertheless important point is that with which all the philosophers grappled — namely, the development of the soul from potentiality to actuality. True, it is, that the reason and the intellect are the tools, so to speak, in raising the soul to the heights of perfectibility. We discussed the questions of theoretical and practical reason; the sensory powers and motor faculties that man and animal possess. We had intimated that, that which is peculiar to man is his rational *soul*. This is in its incipiency, in its potentiality in man — it acts, so to speak, like a "tabula rasa." Therefore, it is called a "hylic intellect," a potential intellect, because it resembles matter which forms

[36] Part I, P. 77, particularly at the end: Of course, Halevi's point is against the above definition of nature insofar as it relates to the item of of prophecy; his argument is that you attribute plurality to God; a new principle cannot propagate itself; nature has strict boundaries. Halevi asks, since you cannot artificially create a new form principle, how can ritual (oil, tefillin) produce a new species? He answers, that it does — the Prophet *is* a new principle. Israel among the nations is just like the heart in a body. Israel has a different disposition, mixture, combination, etc. It takes "Jewish blood" to produce a prophet: only Palestine and Israel can produce a prophet.

[37] Contra Bachya's asceticism. See Part II, p. 50, also Part III, P. 5 and P. 11.

the connecting link between nothingness and actuality, in other words, all potential objects. They obtain rational forms either by way of divine inspiration or by acquisition or application.[38] Original conception with the guidance of nature causes the first and speculation and dialectics are the fields of application. The rational *soul* is the "dynamo," the *motif* of the process from potentiality and passivity to actuality; it is the creative element, giving as Halevi said, a *new form-principle* to man — that is — giving him the possibility of becoming a prophet. The power of the rational soul conceives spontaneously and conceives itself as often as it desires.[39] As matter receives sensible forms so does the material intellect acquire intelligible forms such as thoughts, ideas or concepts — these ideas make the intellect active. — This active reason is nothing more than the abstract of objects conceived, potentially existing in reason itself and rendered actual by it. It is important to note in this connection how significant the inference of self-thought, (and the possibility of self-feeling) and thought thinking thought is (See Note 39). This whole process of creativity, of changing from a state of potentiality to actuality, is an active one, and man, through it, transcends time, plurality sense, and space. He reaches and lives in a world of spirit. Reason chooses those whose natural gifts are perfect, for example, philosophers and those whose souls and character are so harmonious that it can find its dwelling place among the spirits in the dwelling place of God's presence.[40] The divine influence singles out him who appears to have the consciousness and willingness to strive to get himself out of potentiality into actuality and thus receive entrance to God's presence. Divine Providence only gives man

[38] Part V, P. 12: ואמרו במדברת שהיא השכל ההיולני רוצה לומר השכל [בכח] דומה להיולי, אשר היא דומה לאפס בפעל, והוא בדבר בכח, ויהיו בו הצורות המושכלות, אם בלמוד אלהי, ואם בקנין.

[39] Part V, P. 12, pp. 54–55: אבל המשכיל משכיל בעצמו ומשכיל בעצמו בעת שירצה. ועל כן נאמר כי הכח המרגיש מתפעל. והמשכיל פועל: ואין השכל בפועל זולת צורות המושכלות המופשטות בעצם השכל בכח, ולכן נאמר שהשכל בפועל משכיל ומושכל יחד. ומן הכחות המיוחדות לשכל שיאחד הרב וירבה האחד בהרכבה וההתכה. והשכל . . . עצם השכל מרומם מהזמן.

[40] Part II, P. 14.

as much as he is prepared to receive; if his receptivity be small, he obtains little, and much if it be great.[41] The soul, mind, intellect and activity of man must all be attuned towards God and can reach him only if he strives to attain the point of actuality.[42] The divine Influence is beneficent, and desirous of doing good to all. He is always responsive to the receptivity of all who are ready to accept his wisdom, inspiration, light and guidance.[43] A strict individualistic philosophy is herewith presented. It is within the province of each man to win or lose life (and immortality) in accordance with the proper use of his creative functioning, and developmental soul.

[41] Part II P 24, p. 80: כי הענין האלהי איננו חל על האיש אלא כפי הזדמנותו לו אם מעט מעט ואם הרבה הרבה.

[42] Note Bereshith Rabba 29:3.

[43] Part II, P 26, p. 85: אכן הענין האלהי מטיב לכל רוצה הטוב, ובעת שיסתדר דבר ויכון לקבל הנהגתו לא ימנע ממנו להאציל עליו אור וחכמה ודעת — וכאשר יפסד סדרו לא יקבל האור ההוא ויהיה הפסדו. Cf. Part V, P 10. In this, we are forcibly brought back to our premise as stated in the beginning of this thesis.

IX.

ABRAHAM IBN DAUD (c. 1110–c. 1180)

1. *Life and Works.*[1]

With the advent of Abraham ibn Daud there comes upon the horizon in Medieval Jewish philosophy, next to Maimonides, the zenith of individualism in thought, speculation, and research. Ibn Daud was born in the same city as that of Judah Halevi, in Toledo, and he was practically a contemporary of the great poet-philosopher. He descended from a line of scholars. His mother belonged to a family well-known for its learning, and Abraham in early years showed proclivities towards the scientific and philosophical fields. About 1161 he published a chronicle with the name, "Sefer ha-Kabalah" (Book of Tradition). In this he takes Karaism to task and well justifies the chain of tradition which he sought to establish from Moses down to his own day. This work shows a minute array of source material, particularly so, in relation to the time of the Gaonim and the Jews of Spain. Abraham ibn Daud was also interested in Astronomy, having written a book thereon. However, the work for which ibn Daud is best known, and, which had great influence upon students who followed him, is his philosophical treatise, "Emunah Ramoh" (Exalted Faith), written in Arabic in 1168 and preserved in two Hebrew translations: — one by Solomon b. Labi, and the other by Samuel Motot. The former was translated into German.[2] Ibn Daud was not known so much for his original thinking, but, moreso, for his systematization of philosophy up to his day, and, which presentation, influenced

[1] Guttmann, Jacob, *Die Religiöse Philosophie des Abraham ibn Daud aus Toledo*, Göttingen, 1879.

[2] Weil, Simson, publisher, Hebrew and German translation of האמונה הרמה, Frankfurt a. M., 1852. This edition is the one to which textual references will be made.

Maimonides to a great extent. Much of the system employed by Maimonides can be traced to ibn Daud. For example, Hasdai Crescas mentions ibn Daud as the only Jewish philosopher among the predecessors of Maimonides.[3] The classical work of Maimonides completely overshadowed that of ibn Daud, even though the former was greatly indebted to the latter for many valuable suggestions. It may, in truth, be said that much of what ibn Daud had started in philosophical speculation, Maimonides, a noble successor, had finished.

Much of the influence upon ibn Daud was Aristotelian. The only Jewish philosophical works with which ibn Daud had direct contact were Saadia's "Emunoth ve' Deoth" (האמונות והדעות) and Gabirol's "The Fountain of Life" (מקור חיים).[4] Ibn Daud fully recognizes the merits of Saadia, but differs essentially in the treatment of the subject of freedom of the will, which subject forms the chief aim and purpose of his "Emunah Ramah."[5] He spares no words in criticising the above two authors, particularly, "The Fountain of Life" of Gabirol.[6] To a great extent this conflict with Gabirol was natural since ibn Daud may be considered the first real Aristotelian among the Jews, whereas, Gabirol represents the Neo-Platonic philosophy. Ibn Daud attempts strongly to defend the rights of reason and cannot permit any limits to be placed about and around the realms of science, for, to do so, would be to encroach upon the

[3] See Crescas' "Or Adonai," Chapter I, 71b: מורי אברהם בן דאוד, והיה הרב המחבר בספר (הנקרא) מורה הנבוכים נשתמש ברוב הקדמותיהם. Ibn Daud is here mentioned as the only Jewish philosopher among others, who preceded Maimonides.

[4] "Emunah Ramah", *loc. cit.*, p. 2: ולא הגיע אלינו בגלילנו זה ספר הונח בו דבור, יעיר אנשי העיון מזאת האומה אל דבר מהחכמות, זולתי ספר רבינו סעדיה ז"ל, אשר קראו ספר האמונות והדעות, והוא ספר הטיב בו מאד, יגמלנו האל הטוב . . . וגם כן עמדנו על ספר ר' שלמה אבן גבירול ז"ל . . .

[5] *E. R.*, p. 98: ואתה כאשר תבחן פסוקי הגזרה כולם הנה על זה הדרך יצאו כולם. ודע שעל דעת הבחירה היו קדמונינו, האומרים הכל בידי שמים חוץ מיראת שמים, ונמשכ. להם מחכמי הגאונים הביא דבריהם כפשטם, לא יפרשו אותם, אבל האמינו אמתתם. וכאשר תעיין דברי רבינו סעדיה ז"ל בספר האמונות והסברות ודברי זולתו מחכמי האומה תמצאהו כן.

[6] See Kaufman, David, *Studien über Solomon ibn Gabirol*, Budapest, 1899, pp. 108–15; Guttman, J., *Die Philosophie Solomon ibn Gabirol*, Göttingen, 1899, 44 ff.

plan and purpose of the Divine Ruler, who did not give man reason that it should be limited. Philosophy, to ibn Daud, is always to be used with the objective towards harmonizing it with religion: in this manner, religion could be more strengthened and solidified, which religion, Jewish religion, is more preferable. Revelation has made religion and knowledge possible to the Jews, which knowledge only came to other peoples through error and difficulty.[7] In the insistence of the above, namely, to study and do research, ibn Daud differed from his contemporary Judah Halevi. Ibn Daud was cold and analytical in his work and treatment of the various subjects handled — as against the poetic, romantic and passionate treatment of like subjects from the hand and heart of Halevi. The mysticism of others was foreign to ibn Daud, and this is evident in his works and, particularly, in his criticisms of ibn Gabirol.

Ibn Daud will always be known as the first important Jewish philosopher who had a thorough knowledge of Aristotle and his works. He makes a sincere effort to harmonize Aristotelian philosophy with Judaism. Needless to say, the Arabian predecessors and contemporaries were well-known to ibn Daud and he hesitated not to utilize them to the fullest extent, and Maimonides extends upon what ibn Daud had formulated. With these two philosophers, ibn Daud and Maimonides, we reach a turning point in Jewish thought and philosophy, and, what is more important, the minimum and vanishing point of Neo-Platonism. Aristotelianism gets full sway. To ibn Daud reason and knowledge were paramount, and philosophy was to harmonize contradictory currents of thought and authorities, particularly, those currents and authorities of the past, and, the new philosophy, pregnant with Aristotelianism, was deeply intrenched. Ibn Daud was, as philosopher, confronted with this "mass of material" and had an herculean task to systematize the subject matter, a much more difficult task than that of a commentator to Bible or Talmud or the uniting of a novel, dialogue, or poem. It is because of the many cross-currents of

[7] *E. R.*, pp. 62–63: וזה אחר שנששו כעורים אלפי שנים, וטעה מהם מי שטעה ופקר מי שפקר, ברוך שלא נתן חלקינו בהם — אחר כן לא סר האחרון מהם לערער על דעת הראשון.

thought in ibn Daud's day, his desire to put *so much* into such small volume, coupled with the fact of the more popular presentations of his near-contemporaries, as Halevi, Bachya, and Maimonides, that ibn Daud's work, "Emunah Ramah," was not brought forward as to be widely read and discussed.[8]

a) Free-Will

As was stated above, the central point about which ibn Daud's treatise, "Emunah Ramah," centers is that of free-will. This problem, simply stated, is, if human action is determined by God, why does evil, punishment, and the need of prophets exist. There must be some realm over which God has no control if man is really free. The Bible has sufficient sources to prove either side. Reason, however, according to ibn Daud, can harmonize the discrepancies in the Bible, for, we can easily prove that objections to determinism are much greater and with more telling effect than those to freedom. Ibn Daud calls for the study of science, and a research into the knowledge of the attributes and consequences that flow from determinism and freedom. The study of physics and metaphysics will greatly aid in this knowledge, and, the first part of his "Emunah Ramah" is given over to this discussion.[9] At the outset, ibn Daud adjures his readers that his treatise is not easy, and well worth while for beginners in speculative philosophy, who, in the reading of which, may rationalize the tradition of their religion. The truths of the Jewish religion which we receive through tradition, other peoples receive these fundamental principles only after great difficulty extending through thousands of years.[10]

[8] See "Milhamoth Ha-Shem" (ספר מלחמות השם), Levi ben Gerson, pp. 298–328; 328–353; Hebrew text, Leipzig, 1866.

[9] "E. R.," pp. 1 ff.: אמר: שאלת לי, ירוממוך האל, זה שנים על דרוש ההכרח והבחירה, וזכרת לי הרבה שיש לך אחת משתי אלה הקצוות, וזה שהעברות שיעבור עליהן האדם אם האל ית' מכריחו עליהן, אם כן איך יענישו עליהן? או איך יזהיר עליהן בדתות? ועוד אין ישלח נביאיו לצוה עליהן? ...

[10] On p. 4, *E. R.*, Ibn Daud discusses this phase, after quoting from Deut. 4.6: אחר רוב המשא והמתן שעשו בזה אלפי שנים, ולנו אנחנו נתן בלי עמל וחקירה, אבל לקחנוהו מקובל מהנביא האמתי ומצאנוהו מבואר במופת בפלוסופיא האמתית.

b) "Medicine of the Soul"

Ibn Daud was much concerned with the subject of Man — his place, purpose and aim in the whole plan of the universe. In the tri-partite division of his "Emunah Ramah" we find discussions replete with references to clarify this question. The third part in "The Medicine of the Soul" (ברפואת הנפשית)[11] attempts to state the end-all of his whole philosophy concerning Man, a practical treatise, namely, to afford Man happiness.[12] This "quest for happiness" is attained through three channels, namely, by good morals, by proper family life, and, by means of correct social and political conduct. The premise of all of the above is that virtue is the health of the soul and vice is the disease of the soul.[13] In this division of the treatise one sees the use of Plato's psychology[14] in the use of his definitions and classifications with a most evident practical application of Aristotle's "golden mean."[14] Whereas Plato uses as the cardinal virtues, wisdom, courage, and temperance with justice as the harmony of the three virtues, ibn Daud makes justice the virtue of the rational soul.[12] Justice is defined as giving everything, in an impersonal and impartial way, its full due, without excess or defect. In this manner justice assumes its highest stage and affects not only the world without, but, also, the world within man. It is the rational faculty that motivates and operates

[11] The other two major discussions of "Emunah Ramah" are: First part (pp. 1–43): בהקדמת מחכמת הטבע מה שאחריו, והם היותר מעט ממה שיצטרך אליהם משירצה לדעת האמונה הישראלית אחר הסתלק ממדרגת ההמון. Second part (pp. 44–98): בהתחלות הדת.

[12] *E. R.*, p. 98–99: בזה הפרק נבאר שתכלית מה שיגיע אליו בפילוסופיא המעשית הוא הגעת ההצלחה. וזה ישלם בתקון המדות ראשונה, והנהגת הבית שנית, והנימוסים המדיניים שלישית . . . ונאמר ראשונה שנפש האנושית כמו שהיא בעלת שלשה כחות ראשונים גדולים . . . והיושר אם כן הוא ראש המעלות כלן בשלוח. Cf. also "Aboth," I:18.

[13] *E. R.*, p. 102: כי בזה ישיבון נפש כי הנפש כשתרגיש שהיא חוטאת לאל ית' הרבה באולי תתיאש מסליחתו וכפרתו ותחשוב שנצחה אבר ממנה . . . וכאשר תבוא לחדש המעשה יתחדש לו הכוסף לשוב אל האל יתברך.

[14] See Plato's *Republic*, IV, p. 144; 411, Zeller's *Philos. d. Griech.*, II. See Aristotle, *Eth. Nicom.*, IV. Comp. also Saadia's *Emunoth*, X. See Munk's *Mélanges*, p. 389, also Maimonides' *Intr. to Aboth*, IV. Also *E. R.*, p. 98 and note in Guttmann's *loc. cit.*, p. 220 and in re הגדלת הנפש as not being the true "Golden Mean" between תגבורת הכעס and שפלות.

along these lines and brings man to account for indiscretions to his maker.[15] The love of God by man means also to strive to obtain a knowledge of God, of His attributes and actions, of His unbounded love and that no evil can emanate from Him. Ibn Daud discusses all the virtues as they come within the purview and experiences of Man. Thankfulness to God, the fear of Him in majesty and awe, not in the manner of punishment, divine service as a means of habituating a constant thought of God, these, and many other acts and practices of our religion, are only expressions of justice — the highest of all the virtues. The same exhortation to practice is made when ibn Daud discusses the family virtues, the social virtues and the traditional laws which are so misunderstood. Many of the commandments have great subtlety, and, if we are to understand them, we should have faith in executing them even if we do not fully understand them: with this attitude we attain wisdom and, in time, we are able to distinguish between belief and unbelief.[16]

The above give a fair idea of the general themes with which ibn Daud dealt, and, to a great extent many other topics were treated, such as were described in former chapters — common to most all of the medieval students and writers of Jewish philosophy. Ibn Daud did, as has already been pointed out, contribute some new thoughts and these we shall now touch upon, leaving the topic of "Soul" for special emphasis.

c) Substance and Accident

Aristotelian as ibn Daud was, he plunged into a detailed discussion of substance and accident and employs and characterizes the ten categories, showing the Biblical basis for the

[15] Ibn Daud continues this discussion by referring to and applying the "Ten Commandments" and refuting the disinterestedness of God in His people because He had given over the rule of the world to the start — that He and the angels have no further interest in the world. See Guttmann, *loc. cit.*, note pp. 223–225 for interesting discussion and references.

[16] See "E. R.," pp. 98–104; especially, pp. 99 and 100. Ibn Daud closes his book and this discussion with the following, p. 104: הנה אלה תועלות אלה הענינים הדקים המתוקנים בדרך חכמה, שהם ההפרש וההבדל שבין הכפירה והאמונה.

categories.[17] From this discussion he treats the very important subjects of matter and form.[18] His method is truly Aristotelian and his proof of the existence of matter is new. He speaks of primary matter and he says that this is free from all form. There is a common substratum of all things that is subject to change. This matter is at the basis of all change and becoming, and, therefore, could not itself have come through a similar process, for, if such, we should require another matter before it, and, therefore, it would not be the prime matter we thought it to be. This reasoning is truly Aristotelian, and, led Aristotle to the concept of eternal matter, the basis of all becoming and not subject itself to any such process; matter is an ultimate and cannot, therefore, inquire of its origin for all things of the sublunar world originate in matter, and, therefore, since matter is the unoriginated, it is the eternal. Ibn Daud adds his view to the above in saying that even though matter cannot originate as composite objects do in the sublunar world, it does not necessarily follow that it is absolutely ultimate and eternal. God alone is the ultimate and matter is only relative as an ultimate and is itself an effect of God who is the Universal cause. God created matter.[19] Since matter is a relative ultimate to the composite and changeable objects of our world, prime matter, therefore, is the first stage in the process of creation and the next stage would be that this formless matter possesses corporeality in the abstract, thus giving it extension. Ibn Daud then discusses the four elements and their compounds through the stages of mineral, plant, animal and man, and, stresses the fact that the classification and analysis of above, namely, of natural objects, is a logical one rather than a physical one. In reality matter and form exist only as a complete compound.[20]

[17] See *E. R.*," pp. 4–8. Ibn Daud dwells on Psalm 139 in this discussion. The discussion of Soul as substance will be taken up later, as will all interrelated matters to soul and the specific problems treated in passim.

[18] See *E. R.*," pp. 9–13.

[19] *E. R.*, p. 64. Note the important statement: ואחר כן עלו על ידיעת שלשה עצמים בלתי גשמיים, והם החומר המשותף ליסודות הארבעה וכל מורכב מהם.

[20] "E. R.," p. 11: אמנם הוא [החומר הראשון] הוא עצם מושכל, לא נמצא, אמנם ביאור היות הצורה עצם, הנה איך לא תהיה עצם?

d) Motion

A very important part is given to the discussion of MOTION. In this ibn Daud with great cogency prepares a new proof for the existence of God not found in any of the works and writers that went before him. As would be natural he takes it from Aristotle's "Physics." Although ibn Daud does not give Aristotle's general definition of motion (actualization of the potential qua potential) his explanations throughout surely imply it.[21] Ibn Daud states that motion is first connoted with *movement* in place, then, applied to change which is gradual—a sudden change cannot be called motion:[22] the forms within the different things cause motion. The forms determine the kind of motion of the things,[23] — still the thing cannot itself produce the motion, but, rather, an *efficient* cause from without can only cause the motion. The soul and the body are two distinct principles in a living creature — the soul moves the body.[24] A thing cannot move itself because the thing which is moved is potential to the objective which the specific motion is intended to obtain, whereas the thing causing the motion is actual.[25]

e) Infinity

Ibn Daud discusses the topic of infinity as it relates to the proof of the existence of God.[26] He concludes, after several illustrative examples, that there is no infinite line[27] — therefore,

[21] *E. R.*, pp. 13–15.

[22] *E R.*, p. 13: ואחרי כן זה השם נעתק אל כל שינוי יהיה לגשם מעט מעט בדבקות והדרגה, כמו שיגדל מעט מעט או יחסר וזאת התנועה בכמה . . . . וזה כי מה שיהיה מן השנויים פתאום כמו שהשלכנו על מי העפצים מי הקומוס וישתחר פתאום, לא יקרא זה תנועה.

[23] *E. R.*, p. 14: והצורות הם המניעות הראשונות. והנעתם באמצעות המקרים.

[24] *E. R.*, p. 15.

[25] *E. R.*, p. 14: — ולא יתנועעו [היסודות] על הצדדים המתחלפים, בגשמיות או החומר, אם־כן מניע הגשם אינו גשם. וזה שורש גדול ושמור אותו!

[26] *E. R.*, pp. 15–20. — See, in particular, p. 16: ועוד שאם היה גשם בלתי בעל תכלית לא יהיה במקום כלל, לפי כל מה שהוא במקום, שטחי מקום כופים עליו . . . . הנה כבר התבאר שלא יתכן שיהיה גשם בלתי בעל תכלית, ולא נמצאים בפועל בעלי סדור בלתי בעל תכלית.

[27] In this whole discussion, "regressus in infinitum," ibn Daud draws from Aristotle (*Metaphys.* II). He also is in agreement with ibn Sina (cf.

it follows there is no infinite surface or infinite solid, and, following through in this manner of reasoning, there could be no infinite series of objects.[28] The general conclusion is that *infinite number* as an *actuality* is impossible because of evident contradiction in terms (as in the discussion of Motion; to be actual and potential at the same time in the same relation would be a contradiction). Ibn Daud, the strict logician, continues, and proves that no finite body can have infinite power. These principles which ibn Daud deduces, are all important insofar as they help him to prove the existence and incorporeality of God. A knowledge of physics and psychology are both necessary to show that there exist intermediate beings between God and the corporeal substances of the world: these are the angels of the Bible which the philosophers call secondary causes. With this statement, Abraham ibn Daud launches forth into a most detailed and interesting discussion of the *Soul*, which discussion will form the next part of this chapter.[29] The discussion of *Soul* closes the first part of the treatise of "Emunah Ramah." It remains for us, at this point, to briefly survey the second part (the third part on "The Medicine of the Soul" having already been discussed above) of ibn Daud's treatise.[30]

f) God — Existence — Tradition

The first part of "Emunah Ramah" closes with a discussion of the heavenly spheres and their motions.[31] These spheres and

Haarbrucker, *Schahrastani's Religionspartheien und Philosophenschulen*, II, p. 295). Also Bachya ibn Pakuda, *Duties of the Heart*, I, which source may have influenced Spinoza in his *Eth.*, I, Prop. XV.

[28] *E. R.*, p. 16.

[29] *E. R.*, p. 20. Note this very important introductory remark to the study of the soul: בכללים וקבוצים מהחכמה בנפש, נצטרך בזה המהלך אשר אנחנו בדרכו שנבאר שבין הראשון ית' וית' ובין העצמים הגשמיים אמצעיים. וכי כוחותיו ית' מגיעים אל הנבראים הגשמיים בהשתלשלות. ואלה האמצעיים יקראו בלשון התורה מלאכים ובהסכמת הפילוסופים שניים. וזה לא יתבאר במופת אלא מצד תנועת הנפש האנושית מן החסרון אל השלמות, ואם מצד תנועות השמים, עם היות שאנחנו אם נרצה שנביא ראיה על זה, ג"כ מרשמים נמצאים על הגשמים הפחותים מן הבעלי־חיים והצמחים, יהיה אפשר.

[30] *E. R.*, pp. 44–98.

[31] *E. R.*, pp. 41: באשר השמים חיים מדברים ושתנועותיהם תנועות נפשיות ברצון ושכונתם בזה להודות לאל ית'.

stars are regarded as living beings, their motions are voluntary, a result of will and purpose of an unconscious force within them called *Nature*.[32] From this discussion ibn Daud takes up the questions of God, His unity and existence, His attributes and revelation. Ibn Daud proves the existence of a "primum movens immobile" — a first unmoved mover — this is a natural consequence from the discussion on infinity. God being infinite and an unmoved mover, He is not affected by time and, therefore, cannot be body — he is incorporeal. This is new in Jewish philosophy, because ibn Daud's basis of proof is *Motion* — as contrasted to others who base proof upon *Being*.[33] I shall not go into detailed discussion or analysis of this proof, but, suffice it to say that ibn Daud did want to strengthen his stand on the proof of the incorporeality of God from motion.[34] He supplies an additional proof based on the distinction between the "possible" and the "necessary existent" — the former is that which depends upon another and was preceded by non-existence. The latter, "necessary existent," is a thing whose existence is in itself and not derived from elsewhere — God Himself — God the Creator.[35] From the "necessary existent" it follows that God cannot have multiplicity, and He is, therefore, One, and this unity is His essence.[36] In following this discussion through ibn Daud leads us to the topic of divine attributes, and here he offers nothing new. The only attributes he admits in his discus-

[32] *E. R.*, pp. 42–43, Ibn Daud refers to Psalm 19, showing that the spheres praise God with the intellect. וכל מניע גשם הוא אם נפש, אם טבע, הנה מניע השמים אם נפש ואם טבע .... שמן הראוי, שיהיה ערך שכלנו אל שכלי הכוכבים, ערך גודל גשמנו אל גודל גשמיהם וזכות עצמינו אל זכות עצמיהם. Compare *Kuzari* of Halevi, I, pp. 31 ff. and 70 ff.: nature is devoid of intelligence and God alone is intelligence.

[33] *E. R.*, pp. 46–47 and 52 and 61. Compare also Bachya's *Duties of the Heart*, I:5, and Maimonides' *Moreh*, II.

[34] *E. R.*, p. 48: והנמצא אשר מציאותו מחוייב, עצמותו מספיק במציאות עצמותו והנמצא אשר עצמותו מספיק במציאות עצמותו, הוא מחוייב המציאות. כי אם היה קונה המציאות מזולתו היה עצמותו בלתי מספיק במציאות עצמותו וכבר הונח מספיק במציאות עצמותו, הנה והיה מספיק ובלתי מספיק וזה עיקר.

[35] *E. R.*, p. 49. ולא יתלה מציאותו בדבר. ואשר הוא בלתי צריך לדבר וכל דבר צריך אליו. Also see note 3 of Guttmann, *loc. cit.*, p. 120 and notes 1, 2, and 3, p. 122 and note 1, p. 123.

[36] *E. R.*, pp. 47–49 and note 7, p. 125, Guttmann, *loc. cit.*

sion are negative and relative.[37] All anthropomorphisms in the Bible must be understood metaphorically. The most important attributes of God are as follows: One, existent, true, eternal, living, knowing, willing, and able[38] — all of these attributes are in essence, negative.[39] Unity means that there is none like unto Him, and His eternality implies that He is not subject to change or motion; "true" means there is no end and that His existence has no other source. Ibn Daud next takes up the question of proving the existence and nature of intermediate spiritual beings, that is, between God and the corporeal objects of the super and sublunar worlds — in the Bible known as Angels — and, by the philosophers, as secondary causes. The discussion on the "soul" in the second part of this Chapter will have more to say upon this matter of potentiality, but suffice it to say here that the rational soul as actual intermediary agent is the simple substance known as "active Intellect" (רוח הקדש) by the prophets.[40] Ibn Daud then takes up a defense of tradition elaborating on the fields of knowledge, saying that there is an intelligible and a sensible knowledge;[41] — society depends upon knowledge that has come down to us as a social and national heritage, and, particularly, the knowledge that has come to us through prophecy.[42] The Jewish religion has, therefore, developed a "Law," and we find this sum-total of law both rational and traditional. The first is universal: all nations accept them; they are unchangeable as are those laws which are historical in content.[43] Ibn Daud next takes up the problem of evil and of freedom. As to the former, evil, we find ibn Daud relating the subject to a graduated series of imperfections getting less and less imperfect

[37] See Haarbrucker, *loc. cit.*, I, pp. 90–96 for Arabic sources. See *E. R.*, p. 51: רק שהשלילות ואם הם מסלקות ספיקות רבות, אינם מודיעות דבר. Cf. Maimonides, *Moreh*, I:58: יודיעונו דבר בשום דבר מן העצם המבקש ידיעתו מה הוא. Maimonides wants us to know that we may attain a knowledge of God through a knowledge of the negative attributes.

[38] Haarbrucker, *loc. cit.*, I:100; also *E. R.*, p. 56; also *E. R.*, p. 47.

[39] *E. R.*, p. 52: ואשר נשיג זולת אשר לא נשיג בלי ספק.

[40] *E. R.*, pp. 57–69.

[41] *E. R.*, pp. 69–70.

[42] *E. R.*, pp. 70–75.

[43] *E. R.*, pp. 75–81.

graduated series of imperfections getting less and less imperfect as it approaches God, who is perfect and full actuality — and removed entirely from potentiality.[44] It is impossible to think that God has evil or defect and that these should come from Him. Man being composite has the ability to cause good and evil — the one coming from his rational power and the other from the spirited or appetitive: this cannot be said of God who is simple and not composite: therefore, how free then is man in his action?[45] This ibn Daud discusses and says that the acts of man come not under the category of the "necessary" or under that of the "impossible," but under the category of "possible." God *knows* which is of necessity and determined, but this knowledge does not deter man's action or freedom: possibility due to ignorance does not exist in God, but, in man. In this method ibn Daud is quite original and improves upon his predecessors. Ibn Daud insists on the absolute freedom of the will. We shall not enter into a discussion of the details, defects, and shortcomings of ibn Daud's proofs on this still unsolved problem. He does clash with his predecessors, but, suffice it to say, that his method is quite original. From this discussion ibn Daud takes up the Chapter which we reviewed near the beginning of this whole discussion, namely, "The Medicine of the Soul." We are now launching forth to the second large division of our immediate concern, namely, a discussion on the Soul.

2. *The Soul.*

Much more could be said with regard to the topics discussed in the "Emunah Ramah." We should remember that ibn Daud was most original in many of the presentations made with reference to the philosophical and religious subjects analyzed.

[44] *E. R.*, p. 93: עד שיהיה למציאות שני קצוות, קצה לא יצוייר כמוהו בשלמותו וריחוקו והסתלק צד קדושתו מדרכי החסרון כולם, והוא מניע הדברים כלם מבלתי שיתנועע, וקצה לא יצוייר כמוהו בחסרון והרחקתו מצדדי השלמות כלם, והוא מתנועע מן הדברים כלם בסדור ואמצעיים, מבלי שיגיע הוא דבר, וזה אשר קראנוהו היולי.

[45] *E. R.*, pp. 93–98. This part is in answer to the original question and basis of his whole treatise, p. 93, וביאור ההשגחה וסוד היכלת, והוא הפרק אשר בגללו וסבתו הצענו זה הספר והוא היה תחלת המחשבה וסוף המעשה. See reference given of *E. R.*, p. 98 at the beginning of this chapter.

However, only a brief suvey could be given in this chapter. We now come to the specific and special discussion of ibn Daud's, concerning the "soul" — leaving for the "Reflective Analysis" that follows the freedom of picking out some poignant contributions that ibn Daud made to the specific field of "soul-development."

Ibn Daud approaches the discussion of "Soul" after he has completed clarifying the physical doctrines with which he was concerned in the first four main chapters. In his discussion of soul we find the true Aristotelian, and, with equal force, the true logician. The functions of bodies, and, of man particularly, are extra-corporeal in principle and this ibn Daud stresses. Man is different from all others in the animal creation, because, in addition to nutrition, growth, and reproduction, he possesses the faculty of intelligence and appreciates art and has the power of ethical discrimination.[46] It is, therefore, difficult to agree upon the term "soul" since there are so many qualifying factors attached thereto.[47] He falls back to the Aristotelian definition of soul in order to begin building up the whole discussion.[48] Ibn Daud, like most of the philosophers of his day, and, before him, attempts to solve the question of soul — as to whether it is a *substance* or an *accident*.[49] In this discussion he refutes the themes of Hippocrates and Galen, who claimed that the soul is a mixture of the elements,[50] whence comes the conclusion that the soul is a product of this mixture and possibly body itself.[51] This would make soul a phenomenon of the body, an accident, and would deprive the soul of all substantiality, independence, and immortality. Ibn Daud is very insistent and logical in his

[46] *E. R.*, p. 29, where ibn Daud discusses the powers of מדמה ומחשב.

[47] *E. R.*, p. 20: וקראנוהו אנחנו נפש. גזרנו לו זה השם, מפני שהגשמים ונפשו בו, אם בהתנשמות או בהתכה הנעלמת. ואתה אם לא ישר בעיניך זה השם, תשים לו איזה שם שתרצה, כי אין קפידא אצלינו בשמות, אחר שתדע שבקצת הגשמים דבר או דברים אינם גשם.

[48] Arist., *de anima*, II, l. 412, b, 4, and II, l. 412, a, 27 — Soul is "the (first) of a natural body having life potentially."

[49] *E. R.*, p. 21: הנפש שלמות לגשם טבעי בעל חיות בכח.

[50] See Zeller, *Phil. d. Griech.*, III, 1 p. 741. Ibn Daud's reputation shows, unmistakably, ibn Sina's influence.

[51] Compare also *Kuzari*, V:12, as well as Aristotle, *de gener et corrupt*, I, 328a, 10. See *E. R.*, p. 22.

argument against any mechanistic or materialistic theory of the soul as put forth by his predecessors: whereas material and mechanical causes may be evident in the general formation and growth of an animal body, still this is not equally evident in the design or purpose of the individuals of a species: intelligence is present and with a purpose that transcends elemental mixture: this is the soul. This soul is substance and not accident — for, speaking of animals and plants, the accident (Aristotelian) is that which resides *in* a thing but not forming part of it. Ibn Daud insists that soul is substance in the sense in which we apply the term of "form" — which — "specifies" the matter and brings it from potentiality to actuality:[52] it is the efficient and final cause of the body — man (body) exists for the soul and through man and the sublunar world the soul attains perfection, is purified — through science and moral conduct.[52] Ibn Daud discusses the various functions of the various kinds of soul, similar to the manner of the exposition of his predecessors. According to ibn Daud the soul is not eternal — it was created and bestowed upon body and the nature of the mixture within the body determines the kind of a soul that should be connected therewith. The soul does not exist *before* the body — it is "co-being," arising at the same time as the body and in connection therewith, realizing and actualizing the body.[53] The process is an ever on-going process, from seed and sperm to plant and animal. Spheres and stars produce forms (souls) by means of their motions which bring to actuality what is in the living bodies only potentially. However, says ibn Daud, the human soul has

[52] *E. R.*, p. 22: וזה הדבר איננו מזג אשר בהשארותו ישאר המזג, בהעדרו יפסד המזג והגשם אשר היה משא לזה המזג. והדבר אשר יפעל בו יקרא נפש. Also *E. R.*, p. 23: הנה כבר ידעת שהנפש עצם בלתי גשמי, ושהיא עצם בענין צורה ושהיא בגשם המחובר ממנה ומגשם — הוא היולי זה המורכב, נמצאת [במורכב] כחלק ממנו.

This whole discussion of substance and accident is truly Aristotelian, and for the four classes of substance and ibn Sina's influence, see Haarbrucker, *loc. cit.*, II, p. 237, in "Schahrestani." Also Munk, *Mélanges*, p. 363, and Rosin, *loc. cit.*, "Die Ethik des Maimonides," p. 49. Also *E. R.*, p. 25.

[53] *E. R.*, p. 26: וכאשר הגיע הגשם תכליתו או קרוב יתנועע אליו כח ההולדה, ובקש המשגל או ההזרעה כי הפרחים בצמחים כמו ההזרעה בבעלי חיים, והזרעים בהם כמו השכבת זרע בבעלי חיים, ואצל התכלית או בקרוב ממנו תהיה ההולדה, והיא היותר נכבדת ממדרגת הנפש האנושית (הצמחית) . . . וזה המוליד הוא תכלית הנפש הצומחת ושלמותה.

a power not within the realm of other living bodies — namely, the power of grasping intelligibles or universals[54] — to distinguish also between good and evil in all fields of human and social welfare — the powers of a *theoretical* and of a *practical* nature. The SOUL rises gradually to its perfection by using these powers of theoretical nature in understanding the "separate intelligences" of the philosophers and the "secondary causes" as angels in the Bible. With the *practical reason* the soul of man perfects the general relationships of his own self with others in society. From this the soul goes gradually into the highest power in the world of nature, from its obedience to the *practical* reason, which is subservient to the *theoretical* reason and cooperating with the speculative reason — giving rise to the closest communion with the angels of God.[55] The rational power of which ibn Daud speaks is independent of body and, as such, did not exist before the body:[56] it developed into greater strength because of the greater use to which reason is put with the increasing problems that daily confront the rational power. Reason in its perfection is potential in the child, and through divine assistance the first principles of knowledge are attained: there is a continuation — from the simple to the complex, from the known to the unknown.[57] There are three stages in the development of reason, firstly, the "hylic" or potential stage, secondly, the actual intel-

[54] *E. R.*, p. 26: כי הפרחים בצמחים כמו ההזרעה בבעלי חיים וההזרעה בהם כמו השכבת זרע בבעלי חיים.

[55] *E. R.*, p. 32: וג"כ אליו שיוציא המלאכות ויבדיל בין המגונה והנאה במרות והנהגות הבית והמדינה וזה נגלה בלתי צריך לקיים. ולזה היתה הנפש האנושית כאילו היא מתחלקת לשני כחות: כח עיוני, בו תשכיל העצמים הפשוטים והנכבדים אשר יקראו בלשון התורה מלאכים ובלשון הפילוסופים השניים, ושכלים מופשטים — ועוד נקיימם לך מן השכל ומן הכתוב — ובזאת ההבטה אשר לה אל זה הצד, תעלה אל מדרגת השלמות בידיעות מדרגה אחר מדרגה. Also p. 33: וזה הכח הדברי המעשיי יעבוד הכח העיוני מלאכותיי . . . הנה נמצאו מיני הכחות הצמחיות והחיוניות, והכח האנושי המעשיי עובדים הכח האנושי העיוני הוא המדבק בינו ובין המלאכים והאלוה ית' וית'. ואליו הגיעה החכמה ודי לה כי לא ימצא בעולם הטבע כח יותר נכבד מזה ולא כח יעבדהו זה. For a full discussion of ibn Daud's use of חוש המצייר and מדמה ומחשב in addition to the text on p. 29 ff., see Guttmann, *loc. cit.*, pp. 84–93 — the illuminating notes thereto especially.

[56] *E. R.*, p. 34.

[57] *E. R.*, p. 36: כמו שיעלה אדם מכל מה שישיג מחכמת התשבורת אל כל מה שישיג בחכמות התכונה עד שיגיע אל חכמת מדידת הארץ והשמים מבלי שישיגהו בזה לאות או חולשה.

lect, and, thirdly, the acquired intellect.[58] This knowledge leads to a power of forming universals, which power, once attained, the soul, needs not the body for its subsequent existence. More important is the conclusion from the above, namely, that since the soul is not a corporeal power, the death of the body does not cause the extinction of the soul[59] — immortality of the soul is, therefore, an evident conclusion. Ibn Daud concludes his discussion on soul — by showing that metempsychosis is impossible. The soul of man is peculiar to his own elemental mixture — which constitutes the dominant trait — or individuality of his body — therefore, in view of the discussion above, two bodies not identical in all respects cannot be the medium of the same soul.

3. *Reflective Analysis.*

In reflecting upon the foregoing pages relating to Abraham ibn Daud, one cannot but feel the struggle which he had in order to clarify many of the perplexing problems of his day. Of course it was left to Maimonides to bring almost to a zenith and quasi-conclusive plane the many important subjects which ibn Daud had started. Despite the fact that ibn Daud had been influenced tremendously by his contemporaries and immediate predecessors, Arabic and Jewish, still, we sense a keenness and alertness in this, the first true Aristotelian Jewish philosopher. His analytical faculty and unique thoroughness could not but help give an

[58] *E. R.*, p. 37: אחר כך האדם יעלה מן המדרגה הזאת אל הקדים הקדמות ועשיית ההקשים והתלמדות המושכלות מצד הדברים הידועים והיא מדרגה שלישית וכבר הסכימו העם לקרוא שכל האדם קודם הגיעו הראשונות אליו: שכל בכח ולקראת אותו אחר הגיע לו הראשונות שכל בפועל ולקראת אותו אחר הגזע לו החכמות: שכל נקנה ואלה המדרגות לולי הגשם לא יעלה מהשפלה שבהם אל היותר עליונה כלל. See also pp. 60 and 68. Compare Maimonides, *Moreh*, I, P. 72, p. 115a and b, where he uses השכל הנקנה הנאצל, where הנאצל means independent and he developed this thought with שפע which means "overflowing." Note also *Moreh*, III, P. 18, p. 26b, where שכל האנושי is used: Many such places can be noted; also, Halevi makes use of שכל הכללי, the highest power — ability to form universals.

[59] Compare with Saadia, *Emunoth Vedeoth*, IX, P. 2, ואלו הרי יודעין שהגמול איננו כי אם בעולם הזה, איזה דבר נשאר להם אחר שתשרפם האש שיקח אותו? and *E. R.*, p. 39: עם שאנחנו כבר קימנו שהנפש האנושית איננו צורת גשמי כלל.

original turn of mind to problems already treated as well as stimulating his own mind to new and original methods of solving old problems, as well as raising and solving new ones.

It is our province here, in this "Reflective Analysis," to pick out some of the salient features of ibn Daud's treatise as given so meticulously in his "Emunah Ramah." I have given copious references upon most of the topics treated in his book and, here, we shall discuss and apply a few of his thoughts to our own individual selves — trying to see what "developmental" phase in the soul is pertinent to our very life.

At the outset we see that ibn Daud stresses the concepts of potentiality and actuality. He applies these to every part of his treatise where process, generation, development, and action is necessary: the soul, itself, is in need of these, and after proving that soul is substance and not accident — the path for this discussion is much easier. I have already elaborated on this point. Suffice it to say that within each one of us there is a soul, a substance, not an accident, and it behooves us to permit this soul to "specify" us into a personality: to develop our "common clay" from potentiality to actuality. How much more dynamic would our lives be if we could appropriate this thought, and, knowing of the soul-substance within us to strive continually to have it motivate and develop us continually: to let it, in essence, be manifest within ourselves — as the efficient and the final causes of our bodies. Would not our moral conduct — our whole society — our whole knowledge, be more perfect and more productive of good if we but bear in mind that just as the human body is for the soul that it may become perfect through it, so our whole sublunar world would be the medium towards perfecting the human soul. In this sense each one of us contributes to the "over-soul" — and we, as individuals, become dynamic parts of a living and pulsating world.

Cognate to the discussion of above we readily see how immortality would come in for direct treatment. True it is that ibn Daud "dodges" the question, from a logical point of view, of individual immortality. However, I venture here to say that, because of the strong logic in back of his conclusion, namely, that human souls after the death of the body must exist as *One*

Soul, so, therefore, the individual can logically be a part of this *One Soul*. A stick of dynamite, divided into smaller parts, loses none of the "principle" inherent in the functioning of the dynamite.[60] A great difficulty that confronts modern society is that we look for a "limited immortality," sectarian or national, ignoring the pregnant thought that if we but "actualize" our inner-selves towards an unlimited development and improvement of human welfare and conduct that both individuals and society would envisage more readily and easily the source of immortality — the Spirit who gave us all, the "principle" of life eternal. This is very important, in that an individual can attain this unfoldment, this envisaging of immortality through definite stages of development.

Ibn Daud does make a definite contribution in his insistence upon the thought that man can attain immortality, and when the term "man" *is* used, it means not his *body* but something of which his body was the "tool" so to speak. Man's ***reason*** is a unique attainment and does go from potentiality to actuality. The ***perfections*** of the human soul are potentially within us and thus we acquire knowledge — even in its beginnings — which forms the bases of the superstructure of the fundamental principles — these lead to the attainment of the knowledge even of matters, which, at first, were unknown, and lead to the most important content of knowledge, namely, a knowledge of the universals.[61] This knowledge of universals is within the grasp of each one of us and can be made part of our eternal selves: when this knowledge is acquired, the soul needs not the body for its subsequent

[60] See discussion of "God, Soul and Immortality" in P. D. Bookstaber, *Postulates of Perfectibility*.

[61] See *E. R.*, p. 37: ובשכל יחלק מה שלא יחלק בחרב, ובשכל יחובר מה שלא יתחבר באופן מאופני התחבולות, כי השגתו בכל איש מאישי האנשים משותף להם, וכן בכל מין . . . אחר שהדבר המשפיע לצורות ישכיל מה שישפיעהו, וישכילהו מופשט מן החמרים קודם שיתרבו בחמרים, ולהגעת המציאות אשר בפועל להם. אמנם היותם בשכל המשפיע הוא סבה להשפעתם אל החמרים, ולהגעת המציאות אשר בפועל להם, ואין היותם בשכל האדם סבה לזה, וזהו ההפרש שבין שתי ההשגות. וזה היה צד ההכרח אל הגשם האנושי, רצוני שיהיה לו חושים, ילך בהם אל ידיעת הנמצאות הכוללות, ואחר הגיע זה התועלת אין הגשם הכרח בהשארת הנפש, כי אין כל נמצא גשם וכל שכן הנמצאים אשר ישכילו ואין נמצא אחר גשמי ישכיל כלל מצד גשמיותו. וכבר התבאר במה שקדם כי זאת הנפש אשר תשכיל איננו כח מכחות הגשם, וכבר די בזה בשהיא לא תאבד באבדן הגשם, כי מה שהיא זולת דבר אחר לא יתחייב שיאבד באבדו.

existence: the soul being an incorporeal power, the death of the body does not cause the extinction of the soul. This is a very strong structure of logic and reasoning, and, to many of us, upon profound introspection and reflection, there lies herein much stimulating material for soul development. The average man can glean much from just the thought expressed above; still more, can the average man make his life more pulsating with ever-increasing zeal to develop his inner soul towards fullest expression in the fields of knowledge.

Closely allied with the above thought is the stress that ibn Daud puts upon Prophecy. To ibn Daud, Prophecy is primarily concerned with guiding the people in the right way, and such were the prophets of Israel: God, therefore, inspires a proper man as a prophet and enables him to have superior powers — not every man is capable — only one who has a pure soul:[62] the gift is innate and study and the good life help to develop this prophetic gift and power.[63] I feel that this point is very poignant and has a direct bearing upon our own individual selves. An humble life and experience has taught me the possibilities of this thought of ibn Daud — even though, you and I may never attain this goal, surely, a dynamic life brings forth the adumbrations of such prophetic visions within our own souls.[64]

There are two more points which are helpful to us in directing our soul development. Many times in our lives we look for a miracle from God to help us, to bolster up, if you please, our broken and shaken spirits: true, this has been made use of by many religions and peoples. This is not conducive towards building up, towards developing, a dynamic soul. Rather, does ibn Daud exhort us, should we depend, in building up our souls,

[62] *E. R.*, pp. 74–75: וכאשר נשלמו ההתחברויות מן האומה הזמן והמקום, נשפע השפע על המוכן ועל אשר הוא לו בקנין, לא כמו שיושפע על המוטבע. ואין שליחות אל אומה שלא יושגח ביעוד אלהית ומה שדומה לזה.

[63] Note *E. R.*, pp. 74–78. *E. R.*, p. 74: טהרה מביאה לידי נקיות, נקיות מביאה לידי זריזות, זריזות מביאה לידי פרישות, פרישות מביאה לידי רוח הקודש. Compare this with Sotah 9,15; 49b, ‘Ab. Zarah 20b, and Yer. Shek. 3,3. Ibn Daud identifies רוח הקדש with the שכל הפועל — the source of this being in Alfarabi, *Principia*, p. 2: והשכל הפועל הוא אשר ראוי שיאמן בו שהוא הרוח הנאמן והרוח הקדש.

[64] Note *E. R.*, p. 74.

(as has already been explained) upon the intellect. This whole thought and discussion is closely linked up with the discussion of prophecy and tradition. It is because people are dependent upon *outside* forces, rather than upon forces *within* them that we find the lack of true strength of mind and soul. We must remember that miracles had happened in the world, and, prophets may have been the media for them.[65] However, to *depend* upon these as the only means whereby the individual and the soul can attain continuity and development would put the individual and peoples in a sorry plight. Miracles and prophecy are only incidental — and the private and personal character of prophecy and miracle are likewise incidental to the process of establishing the developmental phase of the soul.[66] The goal towards which such process leads is that of an historic consciousness — giving to the personalities and to their activities a definite rational, historic, and traditional certainty.

One of the great difficulties in the world is that which concerns itself with the problem of evil. Many are the impediments towards soul-development because people feel that the evil in the world is God-given. Erroneous as this may be, still we find ourselves pressed for some statement on this phase of our discussion. Ibn Daud does, logically, attack this problem, and, to many of us, we would be safe to let our labors rest with his view and strive diligently in the path he lays out for us. Since we are concerned with soul-development, we find ibn Daud's statement

[65] *E. R.*, p. 71: ולפעמים יפול זה הכח תחת ממשלת השכל מעט והוכנה הנפש המדברת למשוך הנעלם מן העצמים הנכבדים . . . אבל יהיה הוא אשר ישתדל לפגוש העתידות ולהשיבם על הנפש במשלים . . . ואם היו משלי אלה החלומות במה שהיה מיוחד לאיש אחד או בדבר חלקי, לא נאמר שהוא נבואה . . . . ואם היה בדברים הגדולים ומה שיכלול האומות ויתחדש בזמנים הארוכים הוא חלום של נבואה . . . .

[66] *E. R.*, pp. 81: ומופת הנביא אשר דבר בהם פנים בפנים אל המון אומתו והעמידם שהוא עשאם בפני המוניהם כולם, ולא הכזיבוהו בהם שום אדם מהם, ולא הכזיב אותם שום אדם אחריו, — הם הענינים התכופים, והענינים התכופים ראוים שיהיו הקדמות בהקש אמתי המופתי. ויהיה זה מספיק בקיום האמונה האחרונה בע"ה. A very striking utterance: surely in the discussion preceding this, where miracles and prophecy are elaborated upon, ibn Daud desires to impress upon us the weakness into which our Torah would be placed, were it to depend upon for its authority merely the miracles of such private character as the resurrections effected by Elijah and Elisha.

that all defect and evil within us and within the world is the result of the *potential* which has not been aroused into *actuality* of a dynamic and acquired intellect. If we were so to live, feel, and think, as to remove ourselves continually from *potentiality* we would become more perfect and become freer from defect. God's essence is the most perfect, and, since He knows His essence, His is the most perfect knowledge: His perfection is not limited, confined, or stationary, and since it extends and communicates itself to all being in order, so can man appropriate this essence, which is good, and not evil. It is, therefore, impossible that evil should come from God.[67] The defects that we see in life are only privational in character and not positive, and, as such, they are not *made* by anybody: the defects and evils are there because of man's own shortcomings in his development.[68] Ibn Daud has given us a high road to travel and in the spirit of his — yes, his personality — we find a reflex of our own desire, our yearning — looking upwards and onward to attain ever more of the INFINITE . . . We strive incessantly to throw off the shackles of our potentialities — we find ourselves growing more and more away from that *matter* that binds us to the imperfect, the defects of life. As time goes on, we begin to get a part of that wisdom from God — it is *bestowed* upon us from on high upon our rational soul — we begin to feel ourselves a *part* of the oversoul — our soul has developed — the invisible is more visible, — the tangible more tangible, — the unreal — more real.

[67] *E. R.*, pp. 93 f.: ונאמר עתה, שאי אפשר בשום פנים ולא בשום ענין . . . שיצא מהאל יתʼ ויתʼ לא רע ולא חסרון בשום פנים.

[68] *E. R.*, p. 94: והיה רוב הפחיתיות והחסרונות שרשם והתחלתם מחסרון השכל.

X.

MOSES MAIMONIDES (1135–1204)

1. *Life and Works.*

Moses ben Maimon was born in Cordova in 1135. This city was on the decline in prestige, politically and intellectually. When the conditions became unbearable for Jew and Christian alike, Moses' family emigrated from Cordova and went from city to city in Spain and then to Fez in Morocco. Conditions here were not better. They emigrated from here to Acco; he visited Jerusalem and Hebron and then went to old Cairo, Egypt. Here he engaged in the jewel trade with his brother. After the death of his father and brother he decided to study and practice medicine. With great diligence he became most proficient as a physician and he was honored by being appointed physician to the Grand Vizier Alfadhil. He was influential in Jewish circles and was made the spiritual head of the community. He showed himself to be a keen Talmudic student and a most skillful physician and we may say, he was the busiest man of his community.[1] Much introspection, discussion and preliminary drafts for his future work were here wrought. He laid here the foundation of the superstructure of his great philosophic works that were to influence the Jewish religion and thought for centuries to come.

With Maimonides we may truly say that we reach a zenith in Jewish philosophy. He was most comprehensive in his grasp of Jewish tradition, thought and learning. Biblical, Talmudic, Rabbinic, scientific and philosophic learning and sources were at his command. His preliminary learning and preparation were

[1] See "Letters of Maimonides" (. . . אגרות), ed. Amsterdam.

destined to make his writings and utterances not only profound, but of permanent value to all people interested in searching out the truths in the maze of Halacha, Haggada and commentaries of all kind. His purpose was well-defined and towards this end he applied himself with all his inherent acumen and ability of mind and heart and physique. He wanted to harmonize Judaism with philosophy — to reconcile the Bible and Talmud with Aristotle. His interest was in Judaism and to a profound degree, in a rational and enlightened faith.[2] This premise, so to speak, was his guiding star in all of his thoughts and minor writings — he put the seal upon all his efforts with the completion of his masterpiece — namely — the "Guide for the Perplexed" — מורה נבוכים — This book came from the pen of the man, who in his time, was considered the greatest Rabbinic authority. It commanded attention and study because of the man in back of it.— True it is, it created a schism in the Jewish body and there were followers of as well as dissenters from this great man and his work. The theology of Judaism was made to turn about face. He was fully cognizant of the prospective difficulties and he did his best to prepare for them, by strengthening his position with the works that preceded the publication of his "chef d'oeuvre," his — מורה נבוכים.[3]

The commentary to the Mishna and the Talmudic Code known as the "Yad ha-Hazaka" were the two strong antecedents of his great work. In these he showed great learning and, also, received great acclaim from all the Jewish people — he proved to them that he was master of Rabbinic literature. He showed

[2] This is manifest in one of his earliest larger works, namely, the commentary to the Mishna (Introduction to the 11th Chapter of Sanhedrin) which is, in essence, of a harmonizing nature.

[3] Published in Arabic in 1190. — Many editions and translations of this work appeared at various times. The Arabic text and French translation with valuable notes by Solomon Munk, under the title, *Le Guide des Egarés*, 3 volumes, Paris 1856–66. English translation by M. Friedlaender in 3 volumes. London, 1881–85, re-issued in one volume without notes, London, 1910. See: D. Kaufmann, "Der Führer Maimunis in der Weltliteratur," *Archiv für Geschichte der Philosophie*, XI (1898), pp. 335–376.

himself, without doubt, to be the leading authority in Jewish lore and tradition of his day and his influence, after the publication of his Guide, in Arabic and Hebrew, was most widespread.[4] He stands in Jewish thought and religion as Kant does in secular philosophy. Although Abraham ibn Daud anticipated much of Maimuni it took the latter's genius and profound learning to systematize and harmonize all Jewish theories of the past and present and give it force and universality. Maimuni's "Guide for the Perplexed," quite contrary to the purpose of the other works, was written for a special class of persons, for "intellectuals" — for those who were well trained in science and philosophy, not to speak of Bible and Talmud. The work is not a treatise of science or philosophy. These are taken for granted on the part of the reader. A glance through the three parts of the book convinces one immediately that the treatise is apologetic and concordistic at the same time. Aristotelian principles and the philosophy of the Kalam, both are taken up in a most minute and masterly fashion, and woven into Jewish theology. He is master of the art of logic and is able to prove and disprove points that to some seemed unsettled or settled. His method is thoroughgoing and Aristotelian in its essence — particularly is this true in the treatment of the Biblical expressions as metaphors and allegories.[5] He emphasizes the point of proper interpretation of Scriptural "homonyms" and his first part is taken up with this treatment.[6] To Maimuni it is of highest importance. The center and keystone of his whole philosophical system and structure is to teach a sublime spiritual conception of God — God as absolutely incorporeal and without

[4] We should mention the fact that some philosophical and ethical material are also found in his works: 1. *Shemonah Perakin*, (Eight Chapters); Arabic text with German translation by M. Wolff, 2nd edition, Leyden, 1903. 2. Introduction to Ch. 11 of Tal. Sanhedrin. 3. Introduction to sections "Hilcoth Yesode ha-Torah" and Hilcoth Deoth" of the Code.

[5] A striking example is Maimuni's explanation of the term "harlot" in Proverbs 7; the term implies that matter is the cause of evil; also, she is matter without form. Also see his Introduction, pp. 6b–7a.

[6] Aristotle, Philo and ibn Daud used the same term and method.

any resemblance or relation whatsoever to anything else. As was stated above, Maimuni tries to harmonize the Bible and its contents to this spiritual interpretation and the "homonym" is his tool. He feels it very necessary to discuss these in detail and this he does with remarkable success,[7] — after which he is ready to discuss the important theme of divine attributes. All of the above discussion precedes that of the proof of the existence of God — the order, at first, seems, illogical — but with Maimuni (contra Saadia, Bachya, ibn Daud and others) though inversion of treatment is deliberate — he desires to direct his treatment *ad hominem*. The existence of God, to his reading public, was never doubted but they had a very inadequate conception of God's spiritual nature. Homonymous terms have confused the minds of most Jews and it is necessary to start by clarifying the tools of thought and speech. This task Maimuni assumes at the outset — the rest is easy. He endeavors to lead the readers out of darkness by giving them the key to understand fully and truly the vague passages in the Bible.

We cannot go into a detailed discussion of the contents of Maimuni's "Guide" — our treatment is limited to the question of soul — but a few points may be mentioned. Maimuni insisted upon a careful study of nature[8] as necessary to a thorough understanding of the knowledge of God — physics and metaphysics are cognate and should be diligently pursued[9] — despite the difficulties entailed.[10] Maimuni gives minutely the prevailing philosophical views and criticizes them most fairly. He takes the methods of the Mutakallimûn[11] and analyzes their sources and premises and points out their weaknesses. Thus,

[7] Part I, chs. 1, 3–16, 18–30, 37–45, 64–67, 70, the text used is the Warsaw 1872 edition.

[8] III, Ch. 28: "וכבר ידעת מה שבא מחוזק המצוה באהבה, בכל לבבך ובכל נפשך". וכבר בארנו במשנה תורה שזאת האהבה לא־תתכן אלא בהשגת המציאות כלו כפי מה שהוא ובחינת חכמתו בו.

[9] I, Ch. 55: ואמנם יבינהו מי שקדמה לו הידיעה במלאכת ההגיון ובטבע המציאות.

[10] See I, Ch. 34. Some questions raised, for example, regarding the soul: מה היא הנפש — ואיך התחדשה בגוף — ואם נפש האדם תפרד — ואיך תפרד, ובמה זה ואל מה זה.

[11] See introductory chapter of this book.

most of the philosophical concepts are discussed: The Atomic theory, eternity of the world, unity of the universe, motion and time, matter and form, God's unity, existence and corporeality, substance and accident, potentiality and actuality, unity and plurality, and the soul and the supremacy of reason.

2. *The Soul.*

The various topics enumerated above are all interesting and, at the same time, tempting to receive our consideration. We are, however, limited to a few of them in this thesis. For the present we must answer the question, what has Maimuni to say with regard to the *soul*? This is our quest and after answering it we may, in our reflective analysis touch upon some cognate concepts and problems.

To begin with, we may say, that Maimuni, was greatly influenced by the various writers that preceded him — by Aristotelian principles, Neo-Platonic writers, Arabic thought and doctrines. His genius and originality lay in the fact that he carried to a logical conclusion many of the ethical consequences based on the assumptions of his forerunners, like the Greeks and Arabs. Therefore, Maimuni enumerates many of the assumptions of the various philosophers and shows where they have been left undone. He was sure of his ground and his conviction was strong that he even went so far as to put down his ideas into dogmatic form as though they were revelations from Above.[12]

As was stated above, matter and form do play an important part in Maimuni's philosophy as they did with all the others. To him all bodies upon earth are compounded of matter and form.[13] However, form here is not form vulgarly understood, which is the picture and image of the thing, it is "the natural form" — it is the reality of the thing — that by virtue of which it is what it is as distinct from other things which it is not.[14]

[12] Mishna Torah, Hilcoth Yesode ha-Torah, Chs. I–IV.

[13] *Ibid.*, Ch. IV, 2.

[14] I, Ch. 1, p. 12b: אמנם צלם הוא נופל על הצורה הטבעית. ר״ל על הענין אשר בו נתעצם הדבר והיה מה שהוא והוא אמתתו.

In the same chapter we are informed that in man, the "form" is that constituent which gives him human perception[15] and in referring to צלם of Ps. 73:20 he says that "contempt" can only concern the *soul* — that is the specific *form* of man, not the properties and shape of his body.[16] Man's distinctive trait is in his power of intellectual perception[17] which no other creature possesses and this creates his *form*, his differential if I may use this term. This trait in man makes him capable of distinguishing between Matter and Form — despite the fact that matter and form are always together.[18] Maimuni, however, gives a careful analysis of this Aristotelian philosophy particularly when he arrives at the conclusion of the existence of form alone[19] as an intellectual abstraction and principle.[20] Maimuni emphasizes the whole discussion of matter and of form that he leads one into the finest realms, not only of ethics but of metaphysics. In his chapter on control of desires, he says that man has the power to control his bodily wants and earthly desires primarily because he has a unique form.[21] The nature of matter is that form cannot persist in it, but it continually divests itself of one form and takes another. This property of matter gives rise to the element of change and of development, things coming into being and ceasing to be; *form*, on the other hand, does not desire change, and Maimuni says (although we may disagree) that form ceases to be only on account of its connection with matter. He comes to the important conclusion that generic forms are all constant,[22] though they exist in individuals which change —

[15] *Ibid.*

[16] *Ibid.*, p. 13a: ולכן נאמר צלמם תבזה כי הבזיון דבק בנפש אשר היא הצורה המינית, לא לתכונת האיברים ותארם.

[17] *Ibid.*, p. 13b: היא ההשגה השכלית.

[18] Yesode ha-Torah, IV, 7.

[19] II, Ch. 4, p. 17b: אמנם היות הגלגל בעל נפש הוא מבואר עם ההשתכלות. Also, Yesode ha-Torah, IV, 7–8: נפש כל בשר היא צורתו שנתן לו האל.

[20] Aristotle postulates the existence of forms in the upper world which are divorced from matter; these are the "separate intelligences" which emanate one from another and are eternal.

[21] III, Ch. 8, p. 10b–11a: . . . נתן לה ר"ל לצורה האנושית יכולת על החמר וממשלה ושלטון, עד שתכריחהו ותמנע תאוותיו. ותשיבם על מה שאפשר מן היושר והשווי. ומהנה נחלקו מדרגות בני אדם.

[22] *Ibid.*: הלא תראה שהצורות המיניות כלם מתמידות עומדות.

which come and go — but individual form necessarily perish since their existence is only possible in combination with finite matter.

We see at once how easy a step it is to go from *form* to *soul* — it is Aristotelian in essence as was pointed out in connection with the other philosophers studied. Maimuni does emphasize the fact that the soul of all flesh is its form and that the body is the house or the matter in and with which the soul clothes itself.[23] When, therefore, the body which is compounded of the elements, is dissolved, the soul perishes, because it exists only with the body and has no permanent form — and has no permanent existence except *generically* — like other forms.[24]

The soul is one[25] but it has many different faculties, says Maimuni, and this is the reason why philosophers speak of the parts of the soul. This does not mean that the soul is divisible like bodies; they merely enumerate the different faculties. There are five parts of the *soul* — basing this division according to the faculties therein. The nutritive, the sensitive, the imaginative, the emotional, and the rational. This, we see, is in line with the divisions that the other philosophers, (Greek, Arabic, and Jewish) made. Maimuni, however, emphasizes as we have seen intimated in the above, the rational. He says that the first four are common to animals as well as human beings — each faculty functioning in its own peculiar and distinct way — i. e. the emotion of a man is not like that of an ass.[26] The rational soul,[27] the distinctive trait in Man, is that power in man by

[23] Compare III, Ch. 22, p. 33a with this, when Maimuni speaks of Job and his friends and the power of Satan: ... באר שהוא נמנע מלשלוט על הנפש. ושנתן לו שלטון על אלו הדברים הארציים כולם ונבדל בינו ובין הנפש. כלומר שלא נתן לו רשות עליה. והוא אמרו אך את נפשו שמור וכבר בארתי לך שתוף שם נפש בלשוננו ושהוא נופל על הדבר הנשאר מן האדם אחר המות והוא הדבר אשר אין לשטן שלטון עליו. Cf. also I, ch. 41 and see commentary אפודי. Cf. also Aristotle, *de Anima*, II, 1 Ps 4 and 6.

[24] Ysode ha-Torah, IV, 8, 9: נפש כל בשר היא צורתו שנתן לו האל והדעה היתרה המצויה בנפשו של אדם היא צורת האדם השלם בדעתו.

[25] "Eight Chapters," I, pp. 2–8: ... אעלם אן נפס אלאנסאן נפס ואחדה The whole chapter treats of the soul of man and its powers or functions. Cf. *Guide*, III, ch. 12, and Aristotle's *de Anima*, II, 3.

[26] *Ibid.*, p. 4.

[27] *Ibid.*, p. 8.

which he thinks and acquires knowledge and distinguishes between wrong and right actions.[28] In essence, therefore, the soul of man is like the soul of all flesh, simply a form associated with matter having no existence apart from the body. When the body is resolved into its component elements, the soul also perishes with all its parts including the rational. Many commentators however were not satisfied with such conclusion and did not desire to abandon the belief in the survival of the soul. These, accordingly, insisted upon a separate and eternal existence of the rational soul. Maimuni, with his fairness and strict logicality did, however, side with the extremists — but — he went further and, did emphasize the individual as against the rational importance of *soul* (and immortality) — to him the *rational soul* is a potential faculty by virtue of which the possessor is able to create and apprehend ideas.[29] Thus, its cessation and decay is only possible in the event that it does not develop from its potentiality. It is, therefore important for each man to get out of potentiality and make his soul permanent and indestructible.[30] His soul then becomes not a mere function of the body but is really separate and distinct from the body — and, as a result, is not perishable like the body. It persists and perdures for ever like the other "separate intelligences."

The foregoing gives the salient points with regard to the soul-concept of Maimuni. It contains an ethico-religious and rational presentation of the soul, in its matrix of matter and form, in function and in active intelligence. We have, to be sure, important contributions made by this master-intellect of Israel. It remains for us to orientate the soul-concept of Maimuni to the idea of development, and, in this, he has contributed

[28] *Ibid.*, p. 6.

[29] I, P. 72, p. 114a: ומפני זה נמצא בו זה הכח הדברי, אשר בו יחשוב ויסתכל ויעשה . . . ובעבור זה אלו דמית בנפשך אחר מבני אדם נשלל זה הכח מונח עם הכח החיוני לבד, היה אובד לשעתו. וזה הכח נכבד מאד, יותר נכבד מכל כחות בעלי חיים. הוא גם כן נעלם מאד, לא תובן אמתתו בתחלת הדעת המשתתף כהבנת שאר הכחות הטבעיות.

[30] *Guide*, I, P. 70, p. 105a: ומה נכבד זה הענין למי שיבינהו. כי הנשמות הנשארות אחר המות אינה הנשמה ההוה באדם כשיתהוה, שזאת ההוה בעת התהוותו היא כח ההכנה לבד, והדבר הנבדל אחר המות הוא הדבר המגיע בפעל. ולא הנשמה גם כן ההוה הוא הרוח ההוה. ולזה מנו בהוות נשמות ורוחות, אמנם הנבדלות הם דבר אחד בלבד.

much. This we may now take up and it is well to conclude with a reflective glance upon the utterances of this great genius.

3. *Reflective Analysis.*

After carefully studying the utterances of Maimuni, it is well, for our purpose, to reflect upon the essence of his idea of soul and of development. Matter and form stand out preeminently and these we have fully discussed. It remains now to expound briefly and appraise the developmental factor in his philosophy. The outstanding couplet is that of potentiality and actuality, and this, we have found, was emphasized by almost all the other writers. True Aristotelian, as Maimuni was, he made this to include both the lower and higher realms of his ethico-religious process if you please. Reason to Maimuni was the motivating force, the creative and dynamic factor that gave form to man and prompted him to attain that high and exalted position by acquiring that intellect which gave him the right to live on forever.[31] Within this process we have the possibility of man to develop his *soul* to its highest perfection and attain, and win, thereby, immortality. We have referred to this phase of soul development before;[32] the acquired intellect is what we now call "mediation."[33] The mediating factor I choose to add to Maimuni, is a true belief in the Unity of God. The rise from potentiality to actuality can only come through this implicit belief in the existence of God — and — the Active Intellect *per se* is not *the all* in the process — it is to me purposeless if it does not start with the implicit belief in God; this is its guiding star — it relates man to his fellow man and gives him a super-dynamicity, a super-creativity. Although Maimuni does discuss this in his various proofs (the fourth) for the existence of God[34] — he does not "link up," so to speak, the *belief*

[31] For a detailed account of this read, in addition to Maimuni's works, Dr. Scheyer's monograph, *Das Psychologische System des Maimonides*, Frankfurt a. M., 1845.

[32] *Guide*, I, Ps. 70, 72, etc.

[33] See Royce, J., *The World and the Individual.*

[34] *Guide*, II, P. 1.

in the existence of God with his motivating agent — the active intellect — in the process.

We are indebted to Maimuni for a clear analysis of Matter and Form and relating it to man's activity. The former is sin and vice and the latter virtue and goodness. He exhorts us to despise matter and have to do with it only as much as is absolutely necessary.[35] Thus, man obtains a true *form* by acting in the right way — his essential form emerges from potentiality into "the higher knowledge," "the form of the soul" which he has acquired, which he has won by assimilating *ideas* — which are separate from matter.[36] We see here the idea of the two worlds (Greek influence) and it is in the upper world that these "higher forms" of man dwell.[37] This discussion of developing the form of man, his soul, into an "acquired intellect" is important in that these are the elements of struggle, achievement and creativity inherent the process and gives *individual* man a place, an active position in life.

Maimuni, with his customary thoroughness, defines the content and the method of this intellectual process — by which and through which he "wins" the "acquired intellect." We intimated above[38] that this intellect becomes actual and eternal by comprehending the Idea and becoming one with them, it follows, therefore, that the content of the Ideas themselves must be actual and eternal. This is a master-stroke which only a genius like Maimuni can execute. The Ideas, through the apprehension of which the intellect does become active, are

[35] *Ibid.*, III, P. 8.

[36] Yesode ha-Torah, Ch. IV, 8, 9 (quoted previously).

[37] See Yesode ha-Torah, II, 5–6, also note *Guide*, Part III, P. 27, p. 41a, and Albo, *Ikkarim*, III:3. כונת כלל תורה שני דברים, והם תקון הנפש ותקון הגוף... יש לו בו שלמיות. שלמות ראשון והוא שלמות הגוף, ושלמות אחרון והוא שלמות הנפש... ושלמותו האחרון הוא שיהיה משכיל בפועל, והוא שירע כל מה שיכולת האדם לדעתו... ומבואר הוא שזה השלמות האחרון אין בו מעשים ולא מדות, ואמנם הוא דעות לבד,... והוא הנכבד בלא ספק, והוא סבת החיים המתמידים לא זולתו.

[38] *Guide*, I, P. 68, pp. 99a–102a: שהוא השכל והמשכיל והמושכל. ושאלו השלשה הנה כבר התבאר לך כי כשהיה p. 100b: ...עניינים בו ותעלה הם ענין אחד אין רבוי בו השכל נמצא בפעל שהשכל הוא הדבר המושכל. והתבאר שכל שכל פעלו אשר הוא היותו משכיל הוא עצמו. ואם כן השכל והמשכיל והמושכל דבר אחד בעצמו לעולם בכל מה שיושכל בפעל.

those whose content is true and eternal Being[39] — namely — the generic and constant forms, the heavenly bodies, the forms (God and the separate Intelligences) that are free from matter. Such is the *content* but what of the *method* of this intellectual process? Here we are answered by the inherent purpose of the conception itself — namely — the result must be achieved by the intellects own activity[40] — i. e. man must apprehend the truth of Being by rational proofs and must not be satisfied by simply accepting the truth from others by an act of faith — which separates intellect and object and the reason had no part in making the intellect actual.[41]

There remains for us two more points of emphasis — namely that which relates to the ethics of Maimuni and his view of prophecy.

One of the five reasons that Maimuni gives as keeping people away from the study of metaphysics[42] is their natural disposition. He stresses the strong connection between intellectual and moral qualities, they being inter-dependent: the former cannot be perfect unless the latter are.[43] This implies a distinct challenge to man's creativity. His moral qualities must be so constituted that he will be able to diligently prepare himself for the attainment of the highest Intelligence. He must overcome his animal passions and raise himself up to a proximate perfection through the acquisition of wisdom.[44] This is the center of Maimuni's ethics. The question that confronts us now is that of the purpose of human life. This is a topic with which Maimuni deals in a most original and inspiring manner. True, he sets forth individual perfection. Man is to direct his activities (on above moral premise) towards one end — namely — to

[39] Physics and Metaphysics contained all this knowledge.

[40] *Ibid.*, p. 100b.

[41] *Guide*, III, P. 51.

[42] Logic, Physics and the Mathematical sciences were prerequisites.

[43] *Guide*, I, P. 34, p. 54b: והסבה הרבעית ההכנות הטבעיות, וזה שכבר התבאר במופת כי מעלות המדות הם הצעות למעלות הדבריות. ואי אפשר היות דבריות אמתיות ר"ל המושכלות שלמות, אלא לאיש מלומד המדות, בעל נחת וישוב. See also "Eight Chapters," Ch. 2, p. 10, and notes through Ch. B.

[44] Introduction to Commentary on the Mishna.

know God as far as it is possible for man to do so. The Active Intellect is the mediating agent and man must start with this. The highest moral purposes the highest good, if you please, is to fulfill his purpose in life — to know God. All other human activities are incidental aids to preserve man's existence to the end that one activity may be fulfilled[45] — namely — the attainment of the "active intellect." This is, in truth, a transvaluation of values, in which every action has a moral value, good or bad, insofar as it helps or hinders towards the attainment of the *one* purpose. Maimuni does distinguish between "bodily perfection" (perfection of character) and "soul perfection" and the latter to him is "intellectual perfection." Maimuni arrives at his definition of virtue by saying that it is the mean which is equidistant from both extremes[46] — through this his road to the eternal soul is smooth and unhampered.[47] To Maimuni, the "mean," — "virtue," was not an end in itself[48] — it was a sum-total of many separate and distinct "means" in preparation[49] for the supreme moral end. — It is this *end*, the active intellect — that enables us to distinguish between the extremes and the means. This gives rise to two distinct kinds of individuals — namely — the "potential man" and the "actual man." The latter does not come into existence at the start as an independent species, so to speak, but is produced and developed from the first in accordance with a *desire* to develop. It is, therefore, within man's province, to progress in this process — to picture within his soul the true concept of the Idea. I do not agree with Maimuni in his view that the majority of the people who do not become "actual" exist for those who do become "actual." My thesis is more individual — namely — that *each* individual *ought* to know of the possibility of his becoming *actual*

[45] *Ibid.* and *Guide*, III, P. 51 for the discussion of how the perfect worship God — this comprises the studies in preparation for the attainment of the true Idea. See III, Ps. 27 and 54 and Hilcoth Deoth Chs. 3 and 4, for a discussion of the various actions of man as aids towards attaining the true Idea and the true kind of perfection.

[46] Hilchoth Deoth Ch. I; and "Eight Chapters," Ch. 4.

[47] "Eight Chapters," end, cf. p. 30, — Ch. 4, and beginning of Ch. 5.

[48] Quite different than Aristotle's.

[49] *Guide*, III, P. 54.

and, knowing this, wins or loses *life*, *soul*, Intelligence and Immortality.[50] It is the duty of the "actual man" to create within the "potential man" by precept and example, the impetus for study and action. — This our really great perfect men of Israel did — our Fathers and prophets and sages were and are motivating influences.

We are now ready to deal with the most perfect man — the Prophet — he who really obtained a true picture of the Idea, he who has a truly "acquired Intellect."

Prophecy, according to Maimuni, is an inspiration from God which passes through the mediation of the "active Intellect" to the rational power first and then to the faculty of imagination.[51] It is the highest stage a man can attain and *is* open to every one, but this does not mean that everyone attains it. It requires perfection in theoretical wisdom and morals and perfect development of the imaginative power.[52] The varying degrees in the last three perfections give rise to the various degrees of prophets.[53] In accordance with the above, also, we may divide men too insofar as they have the ability of attaining the acquired Intellect. Virtues too are divided into the ethical and intellectual (dianoetic) and man may attain all the virtues through a conscious endeavor to appropriate the active Intellect. Reason, of course, is the supreme attainment and the intellectual virtues are the excellencies of the reason — e. g. science, — which consists in the knowledge of proximate and remote causes of things; pure reason having to do with such innate principles as axioms; the *acquired reason* that obtained through study and action — and all of the above give one a clearness of perception and insight. Thus virtue, if attained through above means, is a permanent and enduring quality of the *soul* occupying an intermediate position between the two extremes, each of which is a vice,[54]

[50] Contra to Introduction to "Zeraim."

[51] Maimuni explains his views on the methods of divine revelation and the nature of prophecy in general and the prophecy of Moses in particular in several places. *Guide*, II, Ps. 32–48. Yesode ha-Torah, Ch. 7.

[52] *Guide*, III, P. 51.

[53] *Guide*, II, P. 45.

[54] *Supra*.

sinning by exceeding the proper measure of the golden mean or falling short of it. The *Prophet,* as such, is that high type of individual, personality, to whom the "golden mean" has always been the path towards God. His *Soul* (and its faculties) has been active and creative throughout life.

XI.

CONCLUSION

We have traversed a long and difficult road in our study of soul-development. It is a different cry and presentation from the eclectic Israeli to the rationalist Maimuni. There are many similarities, as is evident, but these are primarily due to the fact that the concepts with universal import could not, by any fair philosopher, be omitted. We see, however, a thread of continuity in the discussions of the soul concept. Leaving out the pre-existence and the immortality of the soul, we find that practically each philosopher had to give some account of this part of man's life — The concepts of matter and form, potentiality and actuality, "participation," reason and will, Idea and perfection, all had their greater or lesser influence in clarifying or emphasizing the concept of soul. It will be admitted that if you took out the concept of soul in the discussions of the various philosophers you would, thereby, take out the centripetal force of all their systems and utterances, — for — what is the aim and purpose of all their metaphysical theories and doctrines? Is it not concerned with man for whom this world exists? On this basis, then, what can be done for him? This is the undercurrent, and the invisible stream of desire in all the doctrines and theories of the philosophers to teach man how to *develop* his Soul. — We agree he has such unique equipment at birth and we should insist upon man knowing that this soul which he has *in potentia* can be raised and developed into actuality. The content and the method of the process may vary — I personally agree with Maimuni's ethics of the "Golden mean" — but it is common ground that each individual may win or lose the attainment of the true knowledge of God to the extent of which he applies himself to the task of developing his soul. To be sure, we come back to our premise given in the Preface of this book —

namely — the saying of Jeremiah —:כי אם־איש בעונו ימות כל־האדם האכל הבסר תקהינה שניו. "But every one shall die for his own iniquity: every man that eateth the sour grapes, his teeth shall be set on edge" —

True — this is an individualistic philosophy of life: — each man should know that he himself is responsible for his *own* life, for his own *soul*, for his own eternity. With this idea within the hearts and minds of all we surely could feel that a greater freedom and a greater brotherhood would prevail. With greater individual responsibility there will be a concomitant of a greater group responsibility, and peace and good-will will be more prevalent. The Souls of men will harmoniously pulsate towards creating higher, greater and more perfect individuals — finer personalities.